WE ARE ALL FULL OF BATTLECRIES
WE ARE ALL FULL OF BATTLECRIES
WE ARE ALL FULL OF BATTLECRIES
WE ARE ALL FULL OF BATTLECRIES

WE ARE ALL

FULL OF

BATTLECRIES
BATTLECRIES
BATTLECRIES
BATTLECRIES
BATTLECRIES

//AMBER SELQET//

BATTLE(CRIES)
BATTLE(CRIES)
BATTLE(CRIES)

WE ARE ALL FULL OF BATTLECRIES

AMBER SELQET
II

WE ARE ALL FULL OF BATTLECRIES

// **FOR THE NEW WOLVES** //

AMBER SELQET
III

WE ARE ALL FULL OF BATTLECRIES

AMBER SELQET
IV

WE ARE ALL FULL OF BATTLECRIES

1.
"BABY, WHAT'S WRONG?"
SHE SIGHED WITH A SADNESS THAT
PERFORATED MY BONES.

"NOTHING ANYMORE."
HER AIM WAS TRUE.

2.
HER NAME WAS MELANCHOLY
AND I WAS NEVER QUITE THE SAME

3.
I PLANT A DAISY FOR EACH LIFE I RUIN
ACROSS THE LAKE I SEE A FIELD AND CRY IN
THE FACE OF THE UNFAIRNESS OF THE
WORLD

AMBER SELQET
V

4.

BURN THESE CHURCHES DOWN TO THE
GODDAMN GROUND
THEY ARE MOCKERIES OF WHAT THEY CLAIM
TO LOVE

THE ONLY WAY TO HONOUR THE GODS IS
THROUGH ***SACRIFICE AND ACTION,*** SO HERE,
LET ME PRESENT BOTH
AND WHEN THESE PUPPETEERS COLLECT ME
FROM THE SCENE OF THE CRIME
I EXPECT NO MERCY

RESISTANCE IS FUTILE
REBIRTH IS FOREVER

5.

CATACLYSM OF THE HIGHEST ORDER
COMMANDS THEM TOGETHER
CONDEMNING ALL WHO CAME BEFORE
TO SUFFER HAVING SEEN TRUE LOVE
IN A WORLD WHERE IT NEVER AGAIN SHALL BE

WE ARE ALL FULL OF BATTLECRIES

6.
I LONGED FOR YOUR TOUCH
<u>UNTIL I HAD IT</u>
YOUR FINGERTIPS ARE SANDPAPER
THEY HURT ME AS THEY WEAR ME DOWN

7.
I WILL WASH THE ASHES OF YOU OFF MY SKIN
AND THINK OF YOU <u>NEVER</u>
AND BUILD NOTHING HERE

8.
THERE IS COMFORT IN NEW BEGINNINGS
BUT MY VEINS BURN WITH RIGHTEOUS ANGER
AND MY SOUL ACHES FOR JUSTICE IN THE
FORM OF BLOOD

9.
MIRROR, MIRROR ON THE WALL
FUCK OFF

AMBER SELQET
VII

WE ARE ALL FULL OF BATTLECRIES

10.
EACH DUSK SHE SWIMS ACROSS THE RIVER,
TO JOIN THE MAN SHE LOVES
ONE NIGHT THE SEAS PULL HER UNDER,
RAVAGE HER MORTAL SOUL
HE TRIES, BUT CANNOT LIBERATE HER, HIS
OWN IS LOST AS WELL

11.
SHE DRIVES AIMLESSLY
UNSURE WHAT IT IS SHE SEARCHES FOR
REFUSING TO RETURN HOME EMPTY HANDED
HER FAMILY UNCLEAR WHERE THEY WERE
WRONG
WHY ARE THEY NOT ENOUGH?

*SHE WADES THROUGH MUDDIED MEMORIES
AND UNBOUND TRAUMA AND SCREAMS A
FRUSTRATED CRY*

*THE WORLD IS CRUEL AND STILL SHE
CHOOSES NOT TO BE
I TRUST HER WITH MY SOUL*

AMBER SELQET
VIII

12.

THE SUN HITS THE DIRT AND I PRETEND FOR A
MOMENT THAT THAT GLINT IS OF DIAMONDS

WE BOTH KNOW IT'S NOT

HOW IRONIC THAT THIS LIFEBLOOD SPELLS
FEAR
FOR THEY HAVE FORGOTTEN THE WAYS THAT
WERE
AND THESE ARE DEATHS, NOT SACRIFICES
AND THE CRIMSON, THE CRIMSON IS WASTED

ONCE UPON A TIME IT WAS LIQUID DIAMONDS
AND NOW, THEY'RE WASTED IN THE ROUGH

13.

CONFESS TO ME YOUR DARKEST SINS
SO THAT MINE DON'T SEEM SO DEEP

WE ARE ALL FULL OF BATTLECRIES

14.
HIS EYES FILLED WITH REGRET AND HIS
BREATH WARMED
I COULD SEE HIS SOUL MELTING AWAY WITH
HIS WINGS
I WONDER HOW MUCH OF HIS WAX IS STILL IN
THE OCEAN
I WONDER IF THE SUN CARES THAT HE'S
GONE

15.
I TATTOO PASSION ONTO MY SKIN AND HOPE
IT WILL TAKE
AS THE INK BLEEDS DEEPER INTO MY SOUL I
LOSE SIGHT OF WHERE I END OR THE CANVAS
BEGINS

*I WANDER AIMLESSLY AROUND AN ART
GALLERY IN THE HOPES THAT SOMEONE
MIGHT MISTAKE ME FOR A PAINTING*

AMBER SELQET
X

WE ARE ALL FULL OF BATTLECRIES

16.

BLOOD SPILLS OUT, COMMANDING, SUCKING
UP THE LIGHT
IT HAS BEEN TOO LONG, TOO LONG TRAPPED
IN THE DARK
AND NOW IT IS FREE, PRAISE BE

SOMETHING SEEMS A LITTLE OFF
SOON IT DRIES TO NAUGHT
ALL THAT'S LEFT'S A STUPID STAIN, ONE
STUPID GIRL
AND COLD HARD TRUTHS, A HAMMER TO MY
CHEST

17.

THE MARK OF A WEAK MAN
A BLEMISH ON THE SKIN OF A TIRED WOMAN
FOR ONLY THE MOST INSUBSTANTIAL OF
HUMANS WOULD EVER RAISE A HAND TO FEEL
MORE VALID
ENDLESS TORMENT IS A FUCKING PLAGUE ON
THIS EARTH AND THERE'S BY FAR ENOUGH
SADNESS ALREADY WITHOUT YOUR PUNY
INADEQUACY GLARING US IN THE FACE

WE ARE ALL FULL OF BATTLECRIES

18.
"WHY DOES THE LAMB WEEP?"

"FUTILITY."

19.
BLOOD BETWEEN YOUR FINGERS
SICKLY SWEET, JUST LIKE REVENGE
I LAP UP THE SACCHARINE HONEY AND FIND I
AM STILL FAMISHED
THE BLOOD OF THE WICKED TURNS QUICKLY
SOUR AND WILL NOT SOON SATISFY MY
HUNGER FOR MORE

20.
SOME YEARS THE WOUNDS DON'T CLOSE
SOME YEARS CAUTERISE THE SENSATIONS
WHICH REMAIN
THIS YEAR IS A YEAR OF NEW WOUNDS
I KNOW MY SKIN WILL BE TOUGH, MANY
YEARS FROM NOW
WITH MY ARMOUR OF GODDAMN SCARS

21.
HEART IN MY CHEST
BLOOD ON MY SLEEVE

22.
CROSS YOUR HEART AND CLEAR MY HEAD
I WILL NEVER THINK OF THIS MOMENT AGAIN

UNTIL IT'S THREE IN THE MORNING AND I
CAN'T SLEEP
I NEED THE COOL DRAFT BUT SOUNDS OF
AIMLESS TRAFFIC KEEP ME AWAKE
I WISH I HAD SOMEWHERE TO GO AT 3AM

AND SO, I THINK OF YOU, SKIN BLACK WITH
BETRAYAL
AND I WONDER, PERHAPS YOU WERE ALL I
EVER DESERVED
PERHAPS I WAS MORE THAN YOU DID

WE ARE ALL FULL OF BATTLECRIES

23.
HERE LIE ALL THE THINGS I LOVED
BECAUSE I THOUGHT YOU'D LOVE THEM TOO
THANK FUCK YOU DIDN'T
MY MIND IS FREE
AND I CAN REST EASY AT LAST

24.
HE HITS ME

HELP

AGAIN

HELP

HIS FINGER POINTS AT MY CHEST

I STAND ACCUSED

*HE WON'T STAND FOR ANY MORE OF MY
ABUSE*

WE ARE ALL FULL OF BATTLECRIES

25.

LOST BETWEEN THE REEDS AND THE WATER
LILIES FEW
AN HONEST MAN BIDS FAREWELL TO OLD
MORALS ANEW

26.

TERRIFIED STAR GAZER, HOLD A MIRROR TO
THE TRUTH
YOU ARE JUST ONE MORE HOPELESS
DREAMER, TERRIFIED TO ADMIT YOU PINE
OVER THAT WHICH MAY NEVER COME TO
PASS

27.

I GIVE IN AND GRAZE MY LIPS ACROSS THE
NAPE OF HIS NECK, HIS CHEST, HIS LIPS
I AM A FOOL IN DENIAL AND ALL I TASTE IS
DISAPPOINTMENT

WE ARE ALL FULL OF BATTLECRIES

28.
THE NIGHT IS DIM
AND THE STARS SPELL OUT NO WORDS
BUT THEY REMIND ME I CAN NO LONGER GO
TO YOU

29.
WISH UPON AN ATOMIC BOMB
THAT MAYBE YOU'D BE THERE

30.
INTERVIEW
"WHO ARE YOU?"
HE DOESN'T KNOW HIMSELF

31.
VENUS BETWEEN THE WATER LILLIES
BATHED IN SILKY LIGHT
SHE HOLDS A SNAKE
BEWARE WHAT HOLDS YOUR HEART

32.
SAFE HAVEN BUILT ON SERENE WHITE NOISE
THE LAWNMOWER SIGNALS A MAN WHO
CARES
THE OVEN RADIATES DEVOTION

33.
HERE LIES A FOOL FOR LOVE
THE LAST LAUGH GOES TO HIM
I STAND ABOVE, FEELING EMPTY
HIS GRAVE HOLDS A MAN WHOSE HEART WAS
FULL

34.
HELLFIRE CLOAKS MY JEALOUS WORDS
THEY CANNOT BE CONTAINED
I CANNOT STOP BECAUSE DEEP DOWN, I
KNOW, THAT IF I SHUT MY MOUTH
MY MIND WILL BURN
LOST IN ETERNAL , WRETCHED FLAMES

35.

GASOLINE LIGHTS THE MATCH
AND TAKES WITH IT MY HOME

36.

WRAITH UPON THE STAIRWELL, SWATHED IN
JEALOUSY
SHE LONGS FOR LIVING FLESH ONCE MORE,
WHILE SHE BARELY USED HER OWN

37.

GOVERNMENT BRANDED INSPIRATION
HE LOSES AN INCH OF BONE A DAY

38.

FEAR OF MISUNDERSTANDING GUIDES SILENT,
WISTFUL LOVE
ALL THE WHILE, A LONELINESS
TWO CHOSE TO REMAIN SEPARATE IN THE
COLD

AMBER SELQET
XVIII

39.
SO BY MY SIDE IT IS YOU STAND
IN BODY
BUT WHO HAS YOUR SOUL?

40.
THE CASKET OPENS ITSELF UP WIDE
WRAPPED BONES, NEVER BEFORE NEAR
LIGHT
SHE PILLAGES, OF COURSE SHE DOES
IT SHOULD HAVE KNOWN TO STAY CLOSED

41.
UGLY WORDS MASK BEAUTIFUL MOMENTS - A
LIE I TELL MYSELF
I TRY TO CONVINCE MYSELF THINGS ARE NOT
QUITE SO BAD

AMBER SELQET
XIX

WE ARE ALL FULL OF BATTLECRIES

42.
HE DEVOURS HER BEING
BECAUSE YOU ARE WHAT YOU EAT
AND HE WANTS TO BE ADORED
JUST LIKE SHE ADORES HIM

SHE'S DEAD
NOBODY CARES
AND HE'S A PIECE OF SHIT

43.
NO PASSION
JUST REALITY
AND ONE MAN WHO CAN'T BE *FUCKED* TO TRY
HARDER

44.
YOU LOOKED LIKE THE WORLD AND YOU
TALKED LIKE THE SEAS
BUT NOW I KNOW YOU'RE JUST A FUCKING
PUDDLE
AND I HOWL AT THE MOON AS I CONDEMN YOU
FOR THE EMPTINESS IN YOUR EYES

AMBER SELQET
XX

45.
BREATHE IN, BREATHE OUT
LET THE MONSTERS EAT ME WHOLE

46.
I LET YOU BLEED OUT ON THE LAWN
STAY THE FUCK AWAY FROM MY HOME

47.
DIABLO WEPT CRIMSON AS HE TORE INTO THE
FLESH OF THE WICKED

"SAINTS ARE THE BIGGEST SINNERS OF US
ALL."

48.
"WHY WOULD YOU COME HERE?"

"THERE'S ELSEWHERE?"

AMBER SELQET
XXI

49.
UNDER THE MIDNIGHT SHADE SHE MAKES A
PACT WITH THE SELF SHE LEFT BEHIND
SHE DECIDES THE BLOODSHED WAS IN VAIN
NO VICTORIES HERE TODAY

50.
RAW THROAT, BRUISED KNEES
I AM HERE FOR THE HUNGER AND NOTHING
LESS

51.
GARGOYLE ON THE PILLAR
A BATTLE RAGES BELOW
ON PRINCIPLE, NOT PART OF THE FRAY
HESITATION SPELLS DEATH FOR INNOCENCE
TONIGHT

52.
VESSELS OF MINOR HEARTBREAK
ON A ROOFTOP
MAKING ART

53.
PASSION BURNS HER UP

HIS HEART BURNS ALONE AT THE EDGE OF
THE ABYSS

54.
SHE BURNED THE MAPS
SAID ALL COULD BE FOUND WITHIN
I CUT HER WORDS OPEN
WHEN I KNEW HER WORDS WEREN'T TRUE

AMBER SELQET
XXIII

WE ARE ALL FULL OF BATTLECRIES

55.
I AM THE INEVITABLE AND THE ANGERED
I AM THE SCORNED AND THE FLAMES
I AM COME TO YOU IN THE DEPTH OF THE
NIGHT AND I DIG AT YOUR SOUL AND DESTROY
ALL THAT YOU HOLD DEAR
THE SWEET SERENITY OF THE END IS TOO
GENEROUS AN ENDING FOR ONE AS
UNDESERVING AS YOU

I AM NOT A BORN HUNTER BUT THE FLESH OF
YOUR SINS FILES MY TEETH INTO FANGS, MY
CONVICTION INTO ACTION

SOMEWHERE BETWEEN THE BLOOD
SPLATTER AND THE HYPOCRISY I FIND THAT
TRULY, IN THE END, I DON'T CARE
I JUST LONG FOR THE IGNORANCE I ONCE
HELD
I AM NOSTALGIC FOR INNOCENCE AND I RIOT
AT THE WORLD WITH WHITE KNUCKLES AND
INDIGNANT PROSE
I WILL WRITE POEMS IN THE REMNANTS OF
WHAT IS LEFT OF MY SOUL
AND TEND A GARDEN IN THE DESERT
AN OASIS, AWAY FROM YOU

AMBER SELQET
XXIV

56.

THE TRIBUNAL FOR THE FORGOTTEN FINDS
THE ROBES OF THE SAINTS HEAVY WITH THE
BLOOD OF LAMBS

57.

BULLETS SHAPED LIKE LOVE PUNCTURE MY
CHEST AND I FIND I BREATHE LIGHTER AGAIN
I HAD FORGOTTEN, LONG AGO, THE BEAT
AWAKENING AGAINST MY RIBS
I COUGH UP SAND AND IT TASTES LIKE AN
ANCIENT OCEAN
YOU HOLD MY HAND AND WE STAND IN THE
WAVES AND I FEEL THE TWINKLE OF NERVES
THROUGH MY FINGERS
I AM IMPATIENT ONCE AGAIN, TO LIVE, TWICE
AGAIN

58.

HE BITES INTO MY SKIN AND FINDS LIQUORICE
BETWEEN THE CLOUDS
PERHAPS ALL WAS NOT AS ADVERTISED
I SHED A SUIT OF LIES AND FIND I CANNOT
BEGIN TO KNOW WHERE TO START

59.
WALLS STAND BARE
A MAN OF FEW POSSESSIONS AND FEWER
WORDS
BUT WHEN HE SPEAKS
EACH SYLLABLE RINGS TRUE

60.
SHE LIES IN THE BED AS IT SHAKES AGAINST
THE HUM OF THE TRAIN, HEARS THE CHURN
OF WATER DOWN THE FILTHY SHOWER DRAIN
BETWEEN THE TANGLE OF LIMBS AND THE
EXHAUSTION UNDERNEATH THEIR EYES, IT IS
UNCLEAR WHO IS USING WHO

SOMETIMES A MOMENT OF DISTRACTION IS
WORTH GETTING YOUR HEART BROKEN

SOMETIMES FEELING NEEDED IS WORTH ALL
THE PAIN

WE ARE ALL FULL OF BATTLECRIES

61.
WHITE KNUCKLES SURROUND RIFLE
BARRELS, PRISONERS HOPE FOR SAFETY IN
OBSCURITY
A HOWL FROM DEEPER WITHIN THE WOODS,
AT ONCE IT IS A FIRING RANGE, GRATITUDE
REPLACES FEAR
WHIMPER, BAD OMEN, *DISPOSED* - AT ONCE
OLD THREATS RETURN
RED SNOW, ADRENALINE; TERROR HANGS
HEAVY IN THE AIR ONCE MORE

62.
~~STOP~~ YOU'RE HURTING ME
OKAY
THIS IS FINE
I SUPPOSE

63.
FOUR HUNDRED AND THIRTY FIVE SHOWERS
AND STILL I AM NOT CLEAN
I AM STAINED WITH THE FEELING OF YOU
I CAN'T QUITE SHAKE IT
AND I CAN'T HELP BUT HOPE THAT ONE OF
THESE DAYS YOU MIGHT THINK OF ME
AND THE STAIN I LEFT ON YOU

64.
THE DEVIL IS A MOTHER WITH GOOD
INTENTIONS
MISPLACED IN SELFISH ACTIONS

65.
BULLETS BATHED IN SUGAR
SHE SHOOTS
AND HE CRIES A LIFETIME OF SALTY WATER
AND THEY SIT BY THEIR SMALL OCEAN
AND WATCH THE TIDE ROLL IN

WE ARE ALL FULL OF BATTLECRIES

66.
CARING BY OBLIGATION
SHE DOESN'T FEEL A THING
~~A THING~~
~~A THING~~
~~A THING~~

67.
SUCCULENT FRUITS
THE SWEETNESS BURNS MY GUMS
MASKING A THICK SCARLET TREACLE
OOZING FROM THE STEM

68.
SHE SPINS A TALE OF BROKEN THREAD
WEAVES A BLANKET THAT DOES NOUGHT
AND KNOWS IN HER SOUL HER MISTAKES ARE
NOT UNDONE

WE ARE ALL FULL OF BATTLECRIES

69.
NOSTALGIC FOR A PLACE THAT NEVER WAS
WITH PEOPLE THAT NEVER REALLY WERE
AND WE BOTH FUCKING KNOW IT
BUT NEITHER OF US WILL EVER SAY

70.
A PADLOCK ON HIS RIBCAGE
HIS CHEST IS DEFLATING

FUCK

71.
DEJA VU POURS DOWN THE WINDOWS
I FEEL IT NOT
BUT SOMEWHERE, BEYOND, IS A MONSOON

72.
THOSE WHO DO NOT REMEMBER HISTORY
AREN'T DOOMED TO RELIVE IT

AMBER SELQET
XXX

73.

LACERATIONS ALONG YOUR LEGS
THE MOUNTAIN WAS UNKIND
YET, UNDETERRED, HERE YOU STAND
A BLEEDING FIST AROUND A THICKET OF
DESIRE

74.

YOU SLIP THROUGH MY FINGERS
MY CLUMSY HANDS MOVE TOO SLOW
AND I WATCH YOU LEAVE MY LIFE

75.

SHE IS A MARTYR
AND SHE SACRIFICES HER INTEGRITY
FOR MOMENTS OF FLEETING INTIMACY
HIDDEN BETWEEN THE SHEETS OF CASUAL
DISREGARD

AMBER SELQET
XXXI

76.
A SPITEFUL MAN
HE SHAVES HIS LIFE DOWN TO THE BONE
BECAUSE THE BRAWN IS HIS ALONE
AND NOT THE DEVIL'S TO COLLECT

77.
SHOOT THE MESSENGER
DELAY THE INEVITABLE
BATHE IN FUTILITY

78.
DEVOTION IS THE DEVIL
AND THE DEVIL NEVER LIES DORMANT

79.
ONE THOUSAND BRUISES MARK HER LIMBS
EACH ONE A WORD LEFT UNSAID

AMBER SELQET
XXXII

WE ARE ALL FULL OF BATTLECRIES

80.
FOG AT MY WINDOW
TAPPING
IT'S YOU

I COME TO YOU

YOU LEAVE

AT LEAST YOU'RE CONSISTENT

81.
SHE LOOKS LIKE I FEEL
AS THE WIND BLOWS HER AWAY

AMBER SELQET
XXXIII

82.
SACRIFICE YOUR DIGNITY AND LUST FULLY
AFTER ME
WHEN YOUR EYES ARE CLOSED AND THE
SOUNDS ARE MUFFLED AND THERE'S WHISKY
ON YOUR BREATH
I HOPE YOU THINK OF ME AND HOW I TASTE
AND HOW MY FISHNETS LOOK WHEN THEY
ARE RIPPED

83.
SHE PROTECTS HER BODY WITH BARBED
WORDS AND A LONELY HEART

84.
YOU SAY NOTHING
BUT THERE IS NOTHING QUIET ABOUT YOUR
GAZE

WE ARE ALL FULL OF BATTLECRIES

85.

ICE COLD SUGAR
SKIES PUNCTUATED WITH LIGHTS
I AM UNTOUCHABLE

86.

HE IS SMOG, TENDRILS CLASPING AT HER
BODY
CORDS BREACH DEFENCES, HER WORDS DO
NAUGHT
PILLAGING THAT WHICH WAS NOT HIS TO TAKE

SHE LIES BROKEN AMONGST THE ASHES
AND I WATCH THE EMBERS OF HER PSYCHE
TURN COLD

87.

THEY SAY YOU CANNOT HEAR A HEART BREAK
BUT MINE SOUNDS LIKE YOU DRIVING AWAY

WE ARE ALL FULL OF BATTLECRIES

88.
CRUCIFIED ON A BED OF SILENCE
BY THE FAMILY SHE DEFENDS

89.
THINKING ABOUT YOUR HANDS
AROUND MY NECK
OXYGEN ISN'T ALL THAT FUELS ME ANYMORE

90.
TALES FROM THE CRYPT WARNED ME OF YOU
AND I PAID THEM NO HEED

91.
FLAMES TURN INTO EMBERS
BRANCHES BREAK OFF INTO STICKS
CLAY FROM THE FURNACE
REMINDS ME OF WHAT WAS LOST

THANK FUCK

AMBER SELQET
XXXVI

WE ARE ALL FULL OF BATTLECRIES

92.
THE SUN AND MOON, A TRAGEDY
AND ENDLESS CHASE, NO END IN SIGHT

93.
SHE SHEDS HER SKIN, AND WITH IT,
ALL THAT ANCHORED HER TO YOU

94.
HE WONDERS WHEN HE SOLD HIS SOUL
WHAT DID HE GET IN RETURN?

95.
YOUR MIND IS AN AURORA
HAILING ME ACROSS THE SKIES
I LUST TO BE ENVELOPED
IN THE MISTS OF YOUR DARKEST THOUGHTS

WE ARE ALL FULL OF BATTLECRIES

96.
"I PROMISE, MA CHÈRE, THAT I WILL CAPTURE
AND DESTROY YOU.
I WILL BURN YOUR DEFENCES TO THE
GROUND."

97.
HE LEAVES A FIRE IN MY THROAT
MY TONGUE BURNING
A FEVER IN MY BELLY

    AND THEN,

    <u>HE LEAVES ME</u>

98.
I AM DRUNK ON HER TRUST
THE MORE EXPOSED SHE IS
THE GREATER HER DOMINION OVER ME

WE ARE ALL FULL OF BATTLECRIES

99.
I HELD HER DOWN AND WATCHED HER
DROWN
HER FACE TWISTED, SHE CONVULSED
NOTHING ABOUT HER WAS PEACEFUL
AS SHE CHOKED ON MY DECEIT

100.
I COVER MY BODY IN BEAUTIFUL PROSE
IN THE HOPES HE'LL LOOK AT ME
LIKE YOU DID BEFORE WE CAME TO BLOWS

101.
HE BUILT ME A PYRAMID, A SIGN OF HIS
DEVOTION
I GAVE HIM GRATITUDE, IN THE FORM OF
RUNNING WATER
BUT HE WAS GREEDY, AND HE COVETED
MORE
AND BUILT ME NEW PYRAMIDS, EACH ONE
HIGHER THAN THE LAST

SO I GAVE HIM WAR, I GAVE HIM FAMINE
"YOU DON'T CHOOSE WHAT I WILL GIVE YOU"

AMBER SELQET
XXXIX

102.
YOU TASTE ME ON YOUR TONGUE, AND WITH
IT, THE SOURCE OF YOUR SHAME
I AM YOUR DIRTY SECRET, USE ME AS YOU
WISH

103.
YOU REACH OUT AND TOUCH THE SMALL OF
MY BACK AND I AM TREMBLING PETALS AND
NERVOUS SHIVERS
NOBODY HAS BEEN THIS CLOSE SINCE I
RENOUNCED THE GODS
I HAVE NEEDED THIS, TERRIBLY

104.
HE WAS BLEAK NIGHTFALL
COLD TO THE TOUCH
HIS VEINS WERE MADE OF ICICLES
HIS HAIR WAS SHARDS OF GLASS
ASHEN RIBS, CRACKED BONES
FIREPLACE IN A CHEST
BLACKENED WITH YESTERDAYS

AMBER SELQET
XL

WE ARE ALL FULL OF BATTLECRIES

105.

"WHY WON'T YOU FEEL SOMETHING?" HE
SCREAMED
AND GRABBED HER BY THE ARM

"DON'T YOU CARE ENOUGH TO BE ANGRY?" HE
SHRIEKED
SHE COULDN'T FEEL THE HEAT

SHE DOESN'T KNOW HOW TO TELL HIM THAT
SHE HASN'T FELT ALIVE SINCE FOUR YEARS
FROM YESTERDAY

106.

COMPARISON WILL KILL YOU
BUT IT DOES NOT WIELD THE AXE
COMPARISON IS A COWARD'S GAME
BUT, FEAR NOT, MY AIM IS TRUE

107.

I BUILT YOU A GARDEN
LOVE MADE UP THE BARRICADE
AND WHEN YOU SAW IT YOU PRONOUNCED
"WHAT IS THIS MESS YOU'VE MADE?"

AMBER SELQET
XLI

WE ARE ALL FULL OF BATTLECRIES

108.
4 AM, EMPTY STREETS
I THIRST FOR YOU BETWEEN MY SHEETS

6AM, HOME ALONE
I CAN HEAR MY RINGING PHONE

7AM, PHONE RINGS ANEW
AND, AGAIN, I KNOW, STILL IT IS NOT YOU

109.
I LOVE TO WATCH HER TANGO
EACH STEP DRIPS WITH FLAMES
NIL KNOW WHO SHE DANCES FOR
BUT I'M SURE IT ISN'T ME

110.
"WHAT HAS THE WORLD DONE TO YOU?"
I HELD HER IN MY ARMS
"I DID THIS TO MYSELF," SHE SAID
I CRIED ON HER BEHALF

AMBER SELQET
XLII

WE ARE ALL FULL OF BATTLECRIES

111.

THE GUN SPITS BULLETS MADE OF GLASS
AND WHEN THEY SHATTER
A TRIGGER HAD BATHED IN CUTS

112.

THE SERPENT BITES ITS OWN TAIL
AND WELCOMES THE END
FULL CIRCLE

113.

LOST IN THE SOUND OF YOUR EXISTENCE
TWO SETS OF BREATHING MELT INTO ONE
AND I HOLD YOU TIGHT
BEFORE THE SUN CREEPS UP
THIS IS TOO GOOD TO L E T   G   O

114.

THE WORLD BELONGS TO EVERYONE
BUT YOU BELONG TO ME

AMBER SELQET
XLIII

WE ARE ALL FULL OF BATTLECRIES

115.
MAYBE THERE'S A FUTURE
MAYBE THERE'S NOT
MAYBE YOU'VE LOST WHAT YOU HAD OF MINE
GOOD RIDDANCE
<u>BURN IN HELL</u>

116.
WE, DESCENDANTS OF THE SUN
SEEKING THE HEAT IN THE BLOOD OF OTHERS
SO THAT WE MAY FEEL THE WARMTH OF LIFE
AGAIN

WE PLAY PRETEND SO LONG THAT WE BEGIN
TO LOSE OURSELVES

117.
I WISH IT WAS THE THOUGHT OF YOU KEEPING
ME UP
BUT IT'S <u>ANXIETY</u>

WE ARE ALL FULL OF BATTLECRIES

118.
THE UNION OF OUR HEARTS SPELLS DEATH
TO SELFISHNESS
EACH BREATH I BREATHE IS AN ODE TO YOU
A SERENADE FOR ALL TO WHICH I'VE BID
FAREWELL

119.
SHE DESTROYS HERSELF
FOR HIM
HIS CHOICE, AGAIN, NOT HERS

120.
THE ANCIENTS SPEAK OF HUNGER, DESIRE TO
SURVIVE.

BUT THE TRULY IMMORTAL LIVE WITHIN THE
CHAMBERS OF OUR CHEST.

AMBER SELQET
XLV

121.
SHE SIGHS, "THERE REALLY IS NOTHING LIKE
YOUNG LOVE"

I AM DROWNING IN OBSESSION AND YOUR
SPIT IS AN ACID DOWN MY THROAT THAT
REMINDS ME I DON'T YET KNOW HOW TO
LEAVE

I COUGH UP MY RIBS AND MY BODY IS
COLLAPSING AND PERHAPS THIS IS MY TURN
TO BE THE SNAKE IN THE GRASS

I AM MISPLACED SCORN AND I DON'T YET
UNDERSTAND MYSELF

I FIND TWO MORE YOUNG LOVERS BENEATH
AN APPLE TREE AND WISH THEM MY SAME
MISFORTUNES, DEJA VU

122.
THE WICKED NEVER REST
GUILT IS AN INFECTION AND IT CHASES HER
TO RUIN

123.

AND SO IT WAS THAT SHE WAS CARRIED TO
SAFETY
AND THOUGH SHE WAS STAINED WITH HIS
WOES
SHE WAS WHOLE
AND THAT WAS ENOUGH

124.

YOU FALL IN LOVE THE SECOND YOU GET OUT
THE DOOR
YOU COME HOME AND I FIND YOUR EYES
WANDER TO THE WINDOW

IT'S 3AM AND I JUST WANT TO FEEL SOME
WARMTH ON ME
ITS 3AM AND I DON'T KNOW HOW TO ASK YOU
NOT TO LEAVE
I DON'T KNOW HOW TO ASK YOU
FOR A LITTLE LONGER, PLEASE PRETEND

125.
THINK OF ME
THINK OF ME ALWAYS
THINK OF ME WHEN YOU MAKE YOUR FIRST
KILL AND YOU TASTE REGRET AND KNOW IN
YOUR BONES <u>YOU ARE AN IMITATION</u> AND
DEATH WITHOUT MEANING IS WASTEFUL

FOR YOU ARE A WASTEFUL MAN WHOSE
BREATHS LEAK OXYGEN OUT OF THE WORLD
WITHOUT GIVING ANYTHING BACK
AND I CANNOT ALLOW THIS ORDER TO STAY
AS IT IS, IMBALANCED, IMPERFECT
AND NOW THAT YOU HAVE GIVEN IN TO YOUR
WEAKNESS, KILLED ONE UNDESERVING, I CAN
KILL YOU, DESERVING

THE SCALES SIT EVEN ONCE MORE
AND THE PASSION WITHIN ME RETURNS TO
DORMANCY
I PRAY THERE IS MORE VIGOUR IN MY BONES
WHICH WILL YET BE AWOKEN THIS DECADE

WE ARE ALL FULL OF BATTLECRIES

126.
IT'S JULY
AND THE WORLD SMELLS LIKE THE ROSES
WHICH DIED HERE
ALL WHICH REMAINS ARE REMINDERS OF THE
UGLY GASHES, RUNNING DEEP THROUGH THE
MUD

127.
"BEAR ME NO RESENTMENT, FOR IN TRUTH I
LOVE YOU SO."

"IF YOU LOVED ME, WHY DID YOU LET ME GO?"

128.
A SELFISH MAN'S 'I LOVE YOU'S
HELD BACK ON IDLE WHIM

129.
SILHOUETTES INTERTWINED
TWO LIVES REMAIN SEPARATE

AMBER SELQET
XLIX

130.
HOW COULD IT BE, I AM A CYNIC
YET I BELIEVE IN YOU

131.
NUCLEAR FEELINGS
HIS CHEST EXPLODES
LEAVING IN ITS WAKE THE LAST SHROUDS OF
MY DESIRE

132.
THREE HUNDRED AND FIFTY EIGHT REASONS
TO LEAVE
AND I'M STILL HERE, HANDCUFFED TO THE
BED
I SWALLOWED THE ONLY KEY

WE ARE ALL FULL OF BATTLECRIES

133.
HE DOESN'T HAVE THE WORDS TO EXPLAIN
AND SHE DOESN'T HAVE THE PATIENCE TO
WAIT
HE CAN'T THINK OF ONE GOOD REASON SHE
SHOULD HAVE TO
AND YET, HE ASKS HER TO
AND HE KNOWS THE ANSWER'S "YES"
HE WATCHES WITH AN UNFLINCHING RESOLVE
AS HER PETALS WILT ACROSS THEIR
HARDWOOD FLOORS

134.
I BITE INTO HER TO QUICKLY
MY MOUTH FREEZES OVER
MY HEAD ACHES WITH COLD
AND I FEEL NOTHING

135.
NUMB YOUR THOUGHTS
RELEASE YOURSELF INTO THE JAWS OF
NORMALITY
EXISTENCE ISN'T PAINFUL IF YOU DON'T TAKE
PART

AMBER SELQET
LI

WE ARE ALL FULL OF BATTLECRIES

136.
LAY DOWN A HEAD FULL OF SECOND
GUESSES
I RUN MY FINGERS THROUGH YOUR HAIR
WHILE YOU SLEEP
I LEAVE THE DOOR OPEN ON THE WAY OUT
I DON'T WANT TO LEAVE YOU WITH ANY
DOUBT
YOU'RE NOT SAFE, I'VE BEEN HERE
AND I'M ANGRY THAT YOU GET TO REST

137.
THE FREEDOM IS KILLING ME
THERE ARE NO PATHS
JUST ONE EXPANSE
AND SOMEWHERE, OUT THERE, THERE'S YOU

138.
EVOLUTION FOR THE WORST
HIS FLAWS, NOW AN HEIRLOOM
A CROWN OF THORNS TAUNTS HIS GRAVE
A LEGACY BEST FORGOT

AMBER SELQET
LII

139.

TRUST WEIGHS HEAVY ON MY MIND

PLEASE

MAKE IT GO

A W A Y

140.

I JUST WANTED TO LAY DOWN FOR A MINUTE
BUT THE FLOWERS SUNK THEIR ROOTS INTO
MY CHEST
AND I DON'T WANT TO DISRUPT THEIR BLOOM
BUT THIS ISN'T WHERE I WANTED TO BE
I'M LOSING MY MIND AS THEIR ROOTS ARE
GETTING LONG

141.

CLAWS ALONG MY SKULL
TEARING AT MY SANITY
BLURRED THOUGHTS
SOMEWHERE
THE LACERATIONS BEGIN TO FEEL SUBLIME

AMBER SELQET
LIII

142.
TODAY I SAW THE MAN WHO ONCE REDUCED
ME TO A SHELL

I'D LIKE TO SAY HE LOOKED EMPTY
THAT I BROKE A BASEBALL BAT ACROSS HIS
FACE

I STARED ACROSS THE PARKING LOT, A
STRANGER
HE LOOKED ME DEAD IN THE EYES AND I
KNEW RIGHT THEN
AN ORDEAL FOR ME, A TUESDAY FOR HIM
I WAS FORGOTTEN WITH THE REST

143.
I DROP HIM BY THE ROADSIDE
RELIEVED TO LEAVE HIM BEHIND
CONSIGNED TO OBLIVION
REPRESSED FROM WHAT'S LEFT OF MY MIND

144.
I WOULDN'T WISH AN ETERNITY UPON YOU
FOR YOURS IS A HEART SO FRAGILE THAT
MORE THAN ONE LIFETIME OF HEARTACHE
WOULD SURELY BREAK YOU APART

145.
HE BLOWS RASPBERRIES ONTO HER SKIN

THEY BLOSSOM INTO ONE HUNDRED PINK
MEMENTOS

146.
HATE IS REPLACED WITH WORDS OF
SENSELESS RAGE
HE NEEDS HER TO KNOW WHAT SHE HAS
DONE
BUT ALL SHE LEARNS IS
            HE *IS* THE MAN SHE THOUGHT

WE ARE ALL FULL OF BATTLECRIES

147.
SHE HIDES A LIFETIME OF SIN BEHIND "HI"
I HIDE A LIFETIME OF MEDIOCRITY BEHIND
"HELLO"

148.
HE DESTROYS MY HEART AND CALLS IT ART
I SCRATCH HIS CAR AND CALL IT FAR FROM
EVEN

149.
WE ARE A MODERN DAY R AND J
EXCEPT INSTEAD OF POISON AND A BLADE
OUR MUTUAL DESTRUCTION ARRIVES
IN THE FORM OF MORE SELF-DOUBT

150.
HER WORDS, SUSPENDED IN MID AIR
SHE DOESN'T BREATHE
SHE TREMBLES, I COLLAPSE

AMBER SELQET
LVI

WE ARE ALL FULL OF BATTLECRIES

151.
A BABE BORN BY THE OCEAN
HER PARENTS WEPT FOR DAYS

"SHE WILL NEVER TRULY BE OURS"

OWNERSHIP IS THE REQUIREMENT OF A WEAK
SOUL AND GOOD RIDDANCE, THE BABE IS
BETTER OFF WITH NO CHAINS

152.
AND AS SHE SHAVES HER LEGS SHE CRIES
SWEET ECSTASY
THE LAST OF YOU SEEPS DOWN THE DRAIN

153.
"FILL YOUR LUNGS WITH MY PERFUME, FOR I
AM YOUR SALVATION NOW."

154.
"FORGIVE ME NOT, FOR I'M A SINNER.
REALLY, I JUST WANT TO TALK."

155.
ALL YOU HAVE TO OFFER ME
IS A LIFE I'D LOVE TO LIVE
ALL I HAVE TO OFFER YOU
IS WISTFUL WORDS
AND MY SINCEREST SOLACE

156.
SHE SMELLS LIKE MORNING DEW
AND SPEAKS LIKE SUMMER RAIN
SHE MAKES ME FEEL LIKE WINTER
WILL NEVER COME AGAIN

157.
HIS PASSION WAS GRAVE ILLNESS
AND HE ONLY HURTS HIMSELF

AMBER SELQET
LVIII

158.
HOUSE MADE OF IDEAS
IT'S FOUNDATION, PARAPHRASED ANGUISH
SOLITUDE ON HIS TERMS ONLY

159.
SHE REPEATS THE SAME PHRASE EVERY DAY
CONDEMNING ALL THAT HE IS
SHE DOESN'T KNOW HOW TO EXPLAIN
THAT WHILST HER FEELINGS MAY NEVER
CHANGE
THEY CHANGE IN SIZE AND SCOPE

160.
YOU GAVE YOUR WORDS TO ANOTHER
WHY DID THEY NOT COME TO ME FIRST?

WE ARE ALL FULL OF BATTLECRIES

161.
HALF A LIFE, SHAPED AROUND FEAR, REEKING
OF FOREBODING
HE'S LONG GONE, DEAD AND ALONE AND
AFRAID
HIS PICTURE FRAMES AND MEMORIES LEFT
BARREN
IN THE END, I'M NOT SURE HE REMEMBERED
HOW IT FELT TO LIVE
I'M NOT SURE HE REALISED HE WAS DYING

162.
I AM GIDDY
ALL THOUGHTS OVERBOARD
ALL THOUGHTS
EXCEPT FOR YOU

AND WHEN I ARRIVE NO GATES CAN HOLD ME
MY RAGE WILL FORCE ITS WAY IN
AND YOU WILL FACE THE TRUTH OF YOUR
ACTIONS
I AM BECOME YOU
YOU ARE BECOME NAUGHT

WE ARE ALL FULL OF BATTLECRIES

163.
THE PIED PIPER HERE TO COLLECT
DON'T THINK
ACCEPT
THIS IS YOUR NEW CAUSE

164.
A MOTHER'S ARMS
INNOCENCE
SOMETHING SNEAKS BETWEEN THE GAPS
ONE WHOLE LIFE
NO DEFENCE
A BABE ENCASED IN SHADE NO MORE

165.
AS I WANDER THROUGH THE STUDDED SKY
NO NOTION OF FROM WHENCE I CAME
MY HEART BEATS ALONE TONIGHT
AND I THINK IT MAY TOMORROW STILL

AMBER SELQET
LXI

WE ARE ALL FULL OF BATTLECRIES

166.
HIS PUPILS ARE LEAKING
ESCAPING WHAT THEY KNOW
THERE IS NO WORLD OUTSIDE HIS THOUGHTS
HE DECIDES TO LET THIS ONE GO

167.
WHEN THE SUN IS HUNGRY SHE WILL DEVOUR
THESE MEMORIES
LEFT OUT ON THE PAVEMENT TO DIE
ALONG WITH THE FLOWERS YOU NEVER
BOUGHT AND THE SORRIES YOU NEVER SAID
ALL THAT I CONVINCED MYSELF WAS
AFFECTION WILL DIE IN MISERABLE
OBSCURITY
LIKE THE MUNDANE EMPTINESS INSIDE YOUR
CHEST

THIS IS THE LAST BALLAD
THE LAST GOODBYE

AND UP UNTIL YOUR LAST BREATH YOUR
STAGGERING IRRELEVANCE REMAINS TRUE

AMBER SELQET
LXII

168.

WORSHIP ME

TELL ME I'M HOLY AND MAKE SURE YOU MEAN
IT
BATHE ME IN THE LIGHT OF YOUR EMPTINESS
I WOULD EAT YOU ALIVE FIVE TIMES OVER
FOR ONE MORE SECOND OF DIVINE
ABSOLUTION
I MISS MY WINGS ONCE MORE AS I KISS YOU
ETERNAL GOODNIGHT

169.

I RISE WITH THE DEATH OF MY DREAMS
AND FLOAT, AIMLESS IN THE DRAFT

170.

ALICE! ALICE! WHERE DID YOU GO?
AND WHY HAVE YOU LEFT ME HERE ALONE?

WE ARE ALL FULL OF BATTLECRIES

171.
AND SO, THE BLOOD-STAINED SEAS QUIETEN
ONCE MORE
NO LESS RED, BUT MORE TRANSLUCENT
HELD NO LONGER BY SPILLED SOULS AND
RUSTY SCABBARDS
BUT WITHIN THE HULL OF THE SHIP THE
BATTLE NEVER ENDED
THE WAR WITHIN NEVER A WAR WHICH COULD
BE WON

172.
LET'S SEE WHAT I CAN DO WHEN I AM PUSHED
BEYOND THE NET
A LOT, IT TURNS OUT
I BID GOODBYE TO FALSE HOPE AND AN
EMPTY MIND

173.

I STILL REMEMBER THE BITTERNESS OF OUR
FIRST KISS
I ATE ICE CREAM FOR DINNER
MY MOUTH BURNED, STILL
YOU DON'T DESERVE THE ATOMS I LOST
I DON'T DESERVE TO THINK OF YOU WHEN I
EAT ICE CREAM

AND YET, I STILL FUCKING DO

174.

IT LOOKED LIKE DIVINE INTERVENTION WHEN
THE ASHES HIT HIS FACE AND HE MELTED
AWAY INTO THE DIRT
AN ASHEN FAREWELL OF DEEDS LONG DUE
TO BE FORGOT

175.

HADES WRITES HIS OWN END IN SOIL AND
CRIMSON
PLEDGES ALLEGIANCE TO MY DISTRACTED
HEART

WE ARE ALL FULL OF BATTLECRIES

176.
WRITE THE ENDING IN STEEL
EACH BLOW STRENGTHENS MY RESOLVE
AND I KNOW THE OLD ME SHALL DIE THIS DAY
AND LEAVE STRENGTH IN MY DEPARTURE
IN MY CAUSE

177.
PAPER SKIN, INHERITED TRAUMA
THE FATES HAVE BEEN CRUEL
THERE IS CRIMSON AND DIRT IN THE PORES
OF THIS CHILD, SO YOUNG, SO WEAK
I RELEASE HIM FROM PAIN AND GIFT HIM A
SOFTER ENDING

AND I HOWL AT THE DEALER ON BEHALF OF
THESE CARDS THAT WERE DRAWN
HOW IS IT THAT ONE SO YOUNG HAS BEEN
CONDEMNED TO SUFFER SO MUCH
CRUELTY CARES NOT, AND IT REAPS ALL THAT
IT SOWS

AMBER SELQET
LXVI

178.
ODE TO A STUBBORN HEART
I CRY IN THE WAKE OF ALL THAT WAS DONE
AND I HUNT IN THE NAME OF ALL THAT WHICH
WAS ONCE HOLY
NOW BLACK DIRT UNDER MY FINGERNAILS
SCUM

179.
AND SO IT IS THAT WE FASHION OUR OWN
HEAVEN, AND DECIDE OUR OWN HELL
AND CRUCIFY OURSELVES ON THE
CONSTRUCTS OF OUR MORALITY
IN THE HOPES THAT FOR THREE BRIEF
MOMENTS WE MIGHT FIND MEANING
AND WE DO,
      WE DO,
         WE ***DO***

WE ARE ALL FULL OF BATTLECRIES

180.
WE DEFY THE PROPHECIES
SUPERSTITIOUS WEAKNESS CLAD IN FEAR
WE ARE INDOMITABLE, UNTAMED, UNGUIDED
WE ARE ANGRY, FIERCE, AND GREEDY IN
SEARCH OF OUR FUTURES
WE ARE BLOODTHIRSTY WHEN THE MOON IS
WEAK, UNCHANGED WHEN THE MOON IS FULL
OUR FATES ARE UNTETHERED TO THE
MOONS, TO THE ELEMENTS, TO THE RUINS OF
THIS FAITH, WITH GODS WEAKENED BY TIME,
BY SCIENCE

AND WE STAND ON THE ROCKS, TAKE THE
FULL FORCE OF EACH TIDE, AND WE ANCHOR
OURSELVES WITH THE SUM OF OUR WILLS
AND WE DO NOT RUN, THIS DAY OR ANY DAY
YET TO COME

181.
I'M FUCKING ANGRY WHEN I SHOWER AND
THINK OF YOU
OR BEFORE I CROSS THE ROAD
FUCK YOU FOR HURTING ME
FUCK ME FOR CARING
FUCK MY THERAPIST FOR MAKING ME REVISIT
IT, *AGAIN*

AMBER SELQET
LXVIII

182.
I DRINK A HUNDRED SOULS AND STILL THEY
DO NOT FILL THE VOID THAT WAS LEFT

183.
SHE FUCKS ME
SHE FUCKS ME NOT
SHE FUCKS ME
SHE FUCKS ME NOT
SHE FUCKS ME
SHE FUCKS ME OVER

184.
ELECTRIC DREAMS, ELECTRIC VEINS
DARK VOID HEART THAT NAUGHT CAN TOUCH
SHE WAKES AND SEES HUES OF BLUE
BUT IN THE END, STILL IT FADES TO BLACK

WE ARE ALL FULL OF BATTLECRIES

185.
I BUILT A HOUSE ON COTTON CANDY
RAINDROPS SWEPT EVERYTHING AWAY
MY HANDS ARE STICKY WITH THE MISGUIDED
PROMISES I MADE

186.
BROKEN GLASS ON THE WINDOWSILL
BLOOD TRAILS DOWN THE ALLEYWAY
THE VICTIM: THE COFFEEPOT
UPRISING AGAINST BLANKET DEPENDENCE

187.
BACK AGAINST TWO WALLS
MAYBE I DON'T WANT TO FIGHT TODAY

188.
"FORGIVE ME FATHER, FOR MY IMPULSE
I KNOW, YOU'VE SAID IT BEFORE
SELF DEFENCE IS A SIN."

AMBER SELQET
LXX

WE ARE ALL FULL OF BATTLECRIES

189.

THERE IS NO SORROW OF A BROKEN HEART
GREATER THAN MY BLADE

190.

THE SUN SETS ON ANOTHER DAY
BUT I HAVE ALL THE WARMTH I NEED WITH
YOU
MY BLOOD BOILS HOT AND MY VISION RED
YOU'LL RUE THE DAY YOU CONDEMNED MY
BED

191.

SHE FILLS THE VOID WITH THE OCEANS
YET SHE CANNOT TAME THE SEAS
THEY SEEP OUT
SHE IS RENDERED HOLLOW ONCE MORE

SO SHE FILLS THE ABYSS WITH SAND
AND THE SAND ABSORBS LINGERING TIDES
DRYING UP THE LAST OF HER MISTAKES
AND WITH IT, ANY LESSONS LEARNED

WE ARE ALL FULL OF BATTLECRIES

192.
MORNING LIGHT
SHE STILL FEELS VODKA IN HER THROAT
AND IT REMINDS HER SHE WASN'T STRONG
SHE GAVE IN TO WHAT SHE THOUGHT WAS
WRONG

193.
HIS TWIGS MEANT MORE THAN THEIR
BRANCHES
FOR IT WAS ALL HE HAD TO SPARE

194.
I COUNT WEAKNESS WITH EACH OF HER
VICES
I COUNT GRATITUDE WITH EACH STRIDE AWAY

AMBER SELQET
LXXII

195.
THE CRUELEST TRICK THAT WAS EVER
PLAYED
WAS LETTING ME THINK THERE WAS A TRAP
BECAUSE WHEN YOU TOLD ME YOU LOVED ME
IT FELT TOO GOOD TO BE TRUE

AND NOW,

IT'S TRUE NO MORE.

196.
HE DIED OF HEARTBREAK, BROUGHT ON BY
HER DECEIT
SHE WAS BROKEN, HERSELF NO MORE, BODY
SPRAWLED OUT BY HIS GRAVE
THUNDER SOUGHT JUSTICE, AND WITH A
CLAP, SHE WAS CONSUMED
AND TWO BECAME NOT ONE

AMBER SELQET
LXXIII

WE ARE ALL FULL OF BATTLECRIES

197.
EVEN THE DEVIL CRIES FOR BABES

<u>ABANDONED</u>

AT LEAST ORPHANS KNOW THEY WERE LOVED

198.
SHE SUBMITS TO A RUSH OF LUST
TENDRILS FORMED OF SWEET NOTHINGS
HER BODY THRASHES BENEATH THE RIVER

ALL SHE SCREAMS IS "MORE"

199.
BED SHEETS IN SHREDS
PILLOW DESECRATED
MY LUNGS FULL OF FALSE HOPE

AMBER SELQET
LXXIV

WE ARE ALL FULL OF BATTLECRIES

200.
SHE GIVES ME HER BODY ALONG WITH HER
FRAGILE SOUL
"YOU NEEDN'T BE KIND TO ME," SHE SAYS,
"IN FACT, I'D PREFER IT IF YOU WEREN'T"

201.
HE SAYS HER PAINTINGS SHOULD BE SHARED
AND SCORNS HER WHEN SHE SELLS THEM

202.
I AM A RED RAINBOW
AND I WILL DEVOUR THE SKY
BEFORE THE SUN HAS FINISHED SETTING

203.
SHE SINGS A LONELY MELODY OF BROKEN
DREAMS
SHE SPINS A WORLD OF WISHFUL THOUGHTS
WHERE TORMENT IS DULLED BY TIME

AMBER SELQET
LXXV

WE ARE ALL FULL OF BATTLECRIES

204.
WE BOTH KNOW OUR PIECES DON'T FIT

BUT SOMEHOW,
      NOT MATCHING
            BEATS BEING   ALONE

205.
YOU ONLY LOVED ME TO PUT ON A GOOD
SHOW.

I ONLY LEFT YOU TO PUT ON
                A BETTER ONE

206.
YOU ONLY CARE FOR THE PART OF ME THAT
PINES FOR YOU.

AMBER SELQET
LXXVI

WE ARE ALL FULL OF BATTLECRIES

207.
SHE SAID SHE TREASURED ROSES
I ASKED HER WHY
SHE SAID THE THORNS, WHILE HARSH, ARE
BETRAYED BY TENDER PETALS

208.
HIS BED WAS MADE OF STICKS AND STONES
HIS HEART WAS MADE OF FIRE

"THEY ALWAYS DID HURT, YOU KNOW"

THE FLAMES GREW HIGHER AND HIGHER

AMBER SELQET
LXXVII

209.
"WHAT WOULD YOU DO IF I WERE TO PLEDGE
MYSELF TO YOU?"

"WHAT WOULD YOU WANT ME TO DO?"

"PLEDGE YOURSELF BACK."

"WHAT IF I DON'T MEAN IT?"

"LIE."

210.
"I'M SORRY, I LEFT WITHOUT SAYING
GOODBYE."
"YOU DID A LOT OF THINGS WITHOUT SAYING
SORRY."

211.
AS I WAS BLEEDING OUT I CALLED OUT HIS
NAME

"WHAT'S WRONG?"

"WHY CAN'T YOU SEE?"

212.
I AM PARCHED AT THE THOUGHT OF YOU NOT
BEING PARCHED FOR ME.

213.
SHE SAID, "TREAT ME LIKE YOU TREAT THE
WORLD"
BUT I'VE NEVER BEEN OUTSIDE

214.
HE BLEEDS BITTERSWEET COLOURS
AND USES WHAT LITTLE HE HAS LEFT
TO PAINT ME A WORK OF ART

AMBER SELQET
LXXIX

WE ARE ALL FULL OF BATTLECRIES

215.
THE VOID IN HIS SOUL
ATE UP ALL WHO HELD HIM DEAR
AND LEFT HIM STANDING BY THE ROAD
FRIGHTENED BY THE TRAFFIC

216.
I HOLD HIS HAND TIGHTLY
SO THAT HE IS NOT ALONE
BUT MY HAND IS MADE MORNING MIST
AND HE DOESN'T KNOW I'M HERE

217.
IMPALE ME ON YOUR ANTLERS
AND I'LL DIE A HAPPY MAN

218.
DEATH ROLLS DOWN BOTH THEIR ARMS
BANE OF EACH OTHERS' EXISTENCE

AMBER SELQET
LXXX

WE ARE ALL FULL OF BATTLECRIES

219.

I AM RUINED BY THE BEAUTY IN YOUR EYES

220.

BITING COLD, THE LONELY HOURS
WHERE ARE YOU WHEN I REACH OUT?
ARE YOU COMING HOME TO ME?
AM I THE ONLY ONE WHO HOLDS YOU?

I WISH I HADN'T ASKED IN CASE I DO NOT LIKE
THE ANSWER

221.

HE CHOOSES HER
SHE PICKS CONTEMPT
HIS GREEDY HANDS CANNOT MAR HER SKIN
TODAY

WE ARE ALL FULL OF BATTLECRIES

222.
THURSDAY IN THE PARK
HE'S GOT NOWHERE TO GO
FIVE HOURS IN
FIVE MORE, AT LEAST, HE THINKS
WATCHING THROUGH THE WINDOW
OF A CAR THAT HE CALLS HOME
HE WINDS HIS WINDOW UP
ASHAMED OF HOW LIFE NOW IS
STUCK LEFT FIELD
OBLIVION

223.
WALK WITH ME TO THE EDGE OF THE WORLD
WHERE THE PAST MEETS THE PRESENT
LOCK MY HEART AND THROW IT INTO THE
RAVINE
WEEPING HEARTS HELP NO ONE

224.
FORTY PAGES OF REPRESSED DEVOTION
IDEAS ALONE WON'T BUILD A LIFE

AMBER SELQET
LXXXII

WE ARE ALL FULL OF BATTLECRIES

225.
"RIDDLE ME THIS, WHEN DOES THE BATTLE
END?"

THE SPHINX PAUSED A SECOND TO THINK.

"YOU WILL NEVER TRULY BE FREE"

226.
SHE DROPPED HER PILLS ACROSS THE
CARPET
TUMBLED TO HER KNEES

SHE SAID SHE'D EVER BE DEPENDENT
NONETHELESS, HER LIFE IS ABSTRACT ART

227.
HE LEAVES HER WAITING BELOW THE TREE
FOR THEIR LIFE TO BEGIN
HESITATION DOES NOT TEND TO LOVE
THE TREE WITHERS AND DIES

AMBER SELQET
LXXXIII

WE ARE ALL FULL OF BATTLECRIES

228.
HE TRACES MASTERPIECES ON HER BACK
THEY ARE FOR HER, AND HER ALONE

229.
SWEAT FORMING ON MY FACE
MY THROAT AFLAME WITH WORDS I WISH I'D
SAID SOONER
AND YOU TELL ME IT'S TOO LATE
WHY DID I WAIT?

230.
CHEAP HAMBURGER, TINY MEAL
IT'S NOT CEREAL AGAIN
VICTORY IS SOMETIMES SMALL

WE ARE ALL FULL OF BATTLECRIES

231.
THE WAVE BREAKS
AND ANNIHILATES MY WORLD

I HOPE TO GOD
YOU WEREN'T IN TOO MUCH PAIN

232.
SHE LOVED TO MAKE THE THINGS SHE LOVED
SO HE MIGHT LOVE THEM TOO

233.
A MAN DODGES A CANNONBALL
NEAR MISS TO HAPPINESS

234.
YOUR WORDS ONCE FILLED ME, FULL
BUT TODAY THEY ARE MERE WISPS
AND MY STOMACH IS LINED WITH AIR

AMBER SELQET
LXXXV

235.
I RETURNED HOME AT LAST
THE MOMENT I MET YOU

236.
A COMPASS CANNOT AID
WHEN YOU KNOW NOT WHAT YOU SEEK

237.
EMOTIONS ARE A BURDEN
AND THEN, ONE DAY, THEY'RE NOT

238.
THE SUN REMINDS ME OF THE WARMTH IN
THIS WORLD
SO I REACH OUT AND PULL IT FROM YOUR
VEINS

AMBER SELQET
LXXXVI

239.
THE SLATE IS OLD, DIRTY, TARNISHED
STUBBORN, THEY BUILD A LIFE
THE WALLS CRUMBLE AROUND THEM WHILE
THE FOUNDATION ROTS

240.
UNCLAIMED THOUGHTS HANG HEAVY IN THE
AIR
CLUMSY WORDS AND FORCED FEELINGS
BREAKING POINT
THE WAVE HAS NOT YET PASSED

241.
SOLACE IN THE EPISODES OF OTHER
PEOPLE'S LIVES
PROBLEMS ARE PERSONAL ATTACKS WHEN
THEY LAST LONGER THAN THIRTY MINUTES

WE ARE ALL FULL OF BATTLECRIES

242.
TELL ME WHAT I DON'T WANT TO KNOW
SHOVE GROWTH DOWN MY THROAT
DON'T LET ME PROCRASTINATE THE
ACTUALITY OF YOU
AND ALL THAT I ESCAPED

243.
TOMORROW PROMISES AN END

244.
I SAW HER IN MY REAR VIEW MIRROR
I WASN'T GOING TO STOP BUT SHE DIDN'T
LOOK UP
WHY DIDN'T SHE LOOK UP?

245.
"WHY DO YOU ONLY DANCE AT HOME, BUT
NOT WHEN OTHERS ARE NEAR?"

"BECAUSE I DANCE FOR MYSELF ALONE, AND I
AM FULL OF FEAR."

246.
AND I HIT HER SO SHE WOULD KNOW HOW
MUCH I CARE.

AND SHE LEFT SO I WOULD KNOW HOW MUCH
SHE DIDN'T.

247.
I TRACED MY OWN SCARS AND THEY SPELLED
OUT YOUR NAME.

WE ARE ALL FULL OF BATTLECRIES

248.
ETERNALLY FREE FROM HIM
SHE FALLS BACK INTO OLD PATTERNS
SHE CUTS A HOLE IN THE SHAPE OF HIM
AND FILLS IT WITH ANOTHER

SHE TELLS HIM HE IS ALL SHE NEEDS
SO HE CUTS HER OFF FROM THE WORLD
AND ALL SHE CAN THINK AS SHE BLEEDS OUT
"THIS FEELS LIKE DEJA VU"

249.
SHE LOOKS LIKE SPRING
HER SMILE HOLDS ALL THE MELANCHOLY OF
THE WORLD
IT'S SUNDAY AFTERNOON
AT THE BENCH BY THE LAKE
AND SHE WISHES SHE WAS STILL WITH YOU

AMBER SELQET
XC

WE ARE ALL FULL OF BATTLECRIES

250.
THE BATTLE WAS WON.
THE CUTS WERE FRESH.
THE BLOOD NOT YET DRIED.

"IT WASN'T WORTH IT," SHE CRIED.

251.
I AM TERRIFIED OF BEING LOST
I DESPERATELY DO NOT WANT TO BE FOUND

252.
I'D BE HONOURED IF YOU'D LET ME BREAK
YOUR HEART.

AMBER SELQET
XCI

WE ARE ALL FULL OF BATTLECRIES

253.
SHE TOLD ME I COULDN'T HURT HER.

EVIDENCE SAID OTHERWISE, BUT I FEIGNED
IGNORANCE.

AS I SAVOURED THE LAST DROP OF HER, A
TEAR ROLLED DOWN HER CHEEK.

WHEN I TASTED IT I KNEW, THAT SHE KNEW
BETTER TOO.

254.
LET YOUR HEART BLEED ON ME
AND STAIN MY CLOTHES
SO THAT WHEN THIS NIGHT IS OVER
I MAY PRETEND, FOR A MOMENT
YOU NEEDED ME

255.
"WHY DON'T YOU HATE ME?" SHE SCREAMED.

"I WISH I DID. IT WOULD MAKE ALL OF THIS SO
MUCH EASIER."

AMBER SELQET
XCII

WE ARE ALL FULL OF BATTLECRIES

256.
YOU ARE BUT A FOLK TALE
AND YET
I'VE NEVER BEEN SO SURE OF ANYTHING
MI AMOR

257.
"FUCK ME," SHE SAID.

SO I DID.

"TELL ME THAT YOU DON'T CARE."

SO I DID.

"I LOVE YOU."

I DIDN'T CARE.

258.
"I STAINED HIS SHEETS AND HE DECLARED IT
ART. THEN AND THERE, I BECAME HIS."

WE ARE ALL FULL OF BATTLECRIES

259.
TERRIFIED OF DYING
HE HOLDS ON TIGHT TO STRANGERS IN THE
NIGHT
IN THE HOPES A PIECE OF HIMSELF MIGHT
SURVIVE BEYOND THE DAWN

260.
"THERE IS NO ESCAPE FROM ME," HE
ANNOUNCED.

"I HAD TO TRY ANYWAY."

"YOU WEREN'T REALLY TRYING."

261.
HER MIND LEAKS

      A BITTERSWEET SYRUP

I AM UNDONE

      AND YET I AM WHOLE

AMBER SELQET
XCIV

WE ARE ALL FULL OF BATTLECRIES

262.

HE WRITES A STORY IN SWEET SALT WATER
UPON A PAGE THAT NEVER WAS

AND WHEN HE FALLS ASLEEP AT NIGHT
HE STASHES DREAMS UNDER HIS PILLOWS
WHERE THEY STAY FORGOT

263.

HE WAS THE FIRE IN MY THROAT
THE PURPOSE IN MY WORDS
I LOVED HIM SO THAT I HANDED HIM THE HILT
AND I HELD HIS HAND AS HE PLUNGED THE
BLADE

264.

WHAT HAS DIED IN ME WAS THE LAST OF YOU.

AMBER SELQET
XCV

265.
"DON'T CRY FOR ME."

"I WASN'T GOING TO."

266.
DAY SIXTY SEVEN,

I YEARN FOR YOU MORE THAN BEFORE.

267.
HE KEEPS HIS HAND IN HIS POCKET
AND PRETENDS YOU'RE THE REASON
FOR HIS WARMTH

268.
THERE'S NO GLUE TO FIX A BROKEN SPIRIT.

AMBER SELQET
XCVI

269.
A DIZZYING DROP INTO CHAOS
A LIFETIME PASSES US BY
YOU'RE ASLEEP, IT'S SUNDAY MORNING
TOMORROW IS SUNDAY TOO

270.
YOU WREAK HAVOC UPON ALL DOUBTS
THE CRUELTY IN YOUR EYES IS CLEAR TO ME
AND I VOW TO SIPHON PRAYERS FROM YOUR
GREEDY LIPS
AND HUMBLE YOU AND YOUR EXISTENCE OF
NOTHINGS

271.
I DON'T KNOW WHERE TO PUT MY MIND WHEN
WE TALK
SO I TUCK MY FINGERS BETWEEN YOUR
HANDS
SHARE WITH YOU MY THOUGHTS MOST DEAR

THE MORNING SUN BRINGS CLARITY OF
THOUGHTS
I AM HOT WITH REGRET
I DESTROY ALL EVIDENCE AND NEVER SPEAK
TO YOU AGAIN

A YEAR HAS PASSED AND WHEN YOU SIT ON
THE BENCH IN THAT PARK WITH THE SWING
YOU THINK OF OUR SHARED SECRETS AND
PERHAPS ONE DAY WE CAN SHARE ONE
MORE

272.
LOVE IS DESTRUCTION
IT STICKS ITS GREEDY HANDS INTO YOUR
HEART AND TWISTS AND PULLS IT FREE

AND STILL, YOU LUST FOR MORE

WE ARE ALL FULL OF BATTLECRIES

273.
YOU OPEN YOUR MOUTH AND I HEAR WAVES
CRASHING, AND AN OCEAN RIP CONSUMES ME
WHOLE. YOU SOUND LIKE PARADISE AND THE
PATH IS CLEARER IF I JUST FOLLOW YOUR
VOICE TO SHORE.

274.
STRUCTURES CRUMBLE UNDER STRESS
MY HEART BREAKS WITH EVERY BREATH YOU
TAKE
FOR YOU ARE THE STARS AND THE PLANETS
AND THE LIGHT IN THE SKY
YOU ARE THE PAST AND THE FUTURE AND
SHARDS OF OLD MEMORIES

AND STILL, THE BONES OF THIS WORLD WEEP
FOR YOU ARE TOO WEAK TO COMMIT
NOT BRAVE ENOUGH TO CONQUER

YET, I TRUST LIFE WILL BREATHE ACTION INTO
YOU YET
BEFORE YOUR FORTITUDE WAVERS

LET MY PATIENCE NOT BE IN VAIN

AMBER SELQET
XCIX

WE ARE ALL FULL OF BATTLECRIES

275.
I DIDN'T CHOOSE YOU AS A MASTER
AND I NEED NOT BREAK FREE FROM THIS
HERE ILLUSION
YOU ONLY TRICK YOURSELF

276.
AND THE AIR AROUND YOU DANCES WITH AN
INTENSITY BETRAYING YOUR SURFACE
MY LUCK FEELS INFINITE
THAT I SHOULD EVER GET TO EXPERIENCE
YOU

277.
I CAN'T GET ENOUGH OF YOU,

     AND YET,

          I LONG FOR SOLITUDE.

AMBER SELQET
C

278.
"HELP," SHE PLEADS.

I CANNOT GIVE HER WHAT SHE DESERVES.
SHE HAS ASKED THE WRONG MAN.
AND YET I TRY, *SELFISHLY*.

WE ARE ALL FULL OF BATTLECRIES

279.
WE ARE THE ARCHITECTS OF NOTHING
YOU ALONE HAVE DESIGNED THIS HERE
ENDING
AND YOU TOOK IT AWAY FROM ME

I AM STANDING HERE IN A LONG HALLWAY AND
YOU ARE STANDING HERE ACROSS FROM ME
WHY?

YOU TAUNT ME WITH THE HOPE OF FREEDOM
I HAVE NOT YET GATHERED MY STRENGTH
BUT I AM AFLAME WITH CONFUSED HOPES
AND ALTERNATE REALITIES
MY HEALING DOES NOT QUICKEN
MY WOUNDS COME IN THE FORM OF WEAK
BINDINGS AND SECOND GUESSES

<u>MY TIME WILL COME</u>

I AM ANGRY AT THE WORLD
I AM ANGRY AT YOU
I AM ANGRY AT ME
I AM ANGRY
I AM TRUTH AND I AM VENGEANCE AND I WILL
GET MY SHIT TOGETHER IF IT MEANS I CAN
BREAK THESE FALSE BINDINGS AND
CONQUER MORE THAN STALE AIR

SO *I DO, AND I'M ANGRY, AND I DO*

AMBER SELQET
CII

280.
YOU MAY BE DEAD BUT YOU'RE STILL
CHERISHED
YOU MAY BE DEAD BUT I'M STILL YOURS

NOW YOU'RE DEAD AND I THINK OF YOU
OFTEN
NOW YOU'RE DEAD AND I AM IN PIECES
ACROSS THE OCEAN FLOOR

WE ARE ALL FULL OF BATTLECRIES

281.
I KNOW THE DEPTH OF YOUR EMPTINESS AS
YOUR WHISPERS REVERBERATE OFF MY
BONES
YOU'VE WON WARS AGAINST PHARAOHS
YET I, I STEAL THE REDNESS FROM YOUR
BLOOD
AND I MAKE A VOW OF BLOOD THAT I WILL
TAKE THIS HERE PASSION AND SIPHON LIFE
BACK INTO MY OWN HEART

AND YOU DIE
    COLD
    PALE BLOOD

ONLY THE GREEDY DIE WITHOUT PASSION
AND YOU ARE A GLUTTON FOR MORE

WE ARE ALL FULL OF BATTLECRIES

282.
I SEE YOU, AFTERNOON SUN IN YOUR HAIR,
WRAPPED IN THE REMNANTS OF A WARM
SIESTA.

I SEE YOU, SPRAWLED OUT, LAZY SMILE
DANCING AT THE CORNER OF YOUR MOUTH,
MORE HANDSOME EACH TOMORROW.

I SEE YOU, EYES ON THE WORLD, SOUL
LEAKING OUT, HAND ON MY THIGH.

I SEE YOU AND I'M IN LOVE.

AND THE WARMTH OF THE SUN FEELS LIKE
YOUR TOUCH, AND IN ALL THE TOMORROWS I
WON'T RUN OUT OF LOVE, AND THE WORLD IS
YOURS AND I WILL GIVE YOU THE SEAS OF MY
SOUL FIVE THOUSAND TIMES OVER, WITH
BLATANT DISREGARD FOR THE TREES WHICH
WENT INTO THESE PAGES.

I LOVE YOU, WITH ALL THE ABUNDANCE OF
TOMORROW.

AMBER SELQET
CV

WE ARE ALL FULL OF BATTLECRIES

283.
ENDLESS MAZE OF CLAY AND STONE
LABYRINTH WITH A CROWN IN MIND
PRISONER WITHIN YOUR OWN CREATION
ESCAPE IN EXCHANGE FOR MELTED WAX
SWEET DAEDALUS, WITH TEARS LIKE
ENDLESS SNOW
ICARUS HAS FLOWN TOO AWAY
IT'S NOT YET YOUR TIME TO FOLLOW

284.
STANDING ON THE GRAVES OF THE
FOREFATHERS OF YOUR FATHERS
ANCIENT WINDS MEET UNMARKED SKIN
GO FREE, THEY CHANT
BREAK CHAINS, THEY CHANT

A NEW STAKE CLAIMS OLD GROUND AND YET
ANOTHER GENERATION IS CLAIMED BY THE
HARSHNESS OF THIS LAND
IN VAIN
IN VAIN
IN VAIN

AMBER SELQET
CVI

WE ARE ALL FULL OF BATTLECRIES

285.
BANSHEES DROWN IN THE RIVER
BOLD TOO SOON, TWO WRAITHS REMAIN
A CUNNING MAN, A BRIDE AT HOME WHO
WAITS

HE IS SURE HE WILL RETURN THIS NIGHT

THE WRAITHS ARE LURED TO HOLY GROUND
BY VIRGIN FLESH AND WHISPERED TONES
<u>CONSECRATE THEM WHERE THEY STAND</u>
LET THEM GIVE CHASE TO THE FERRYMAN
AS THEY DANCE THEIR WAY TO DEATH

286.
THREE BROTHERS, THREE SWORDS
ONE SIBLING ALONE, SWEATING UNDER
HARSH SUN
ONE SIBLING ALONE, TALKING ABOUT
TOMORROW WITH THE MOON
AND THE BLOOD MOON RISES WITH THE HILTS
OF JEALOUS BLADES
TWO BROTHERS, THREE SWORDS
ONE BROTHER, DEAD

287.
THE MUDDIED STEPS OF VALHALLA
OVERFLOW WITH THE LOST TALES OF
BATTLES NEARLY FOUGHT
I STEP OVER BROKEN HORSES AND BLADES
SHARP WITH ANTICIPATION
THESE HERE ARE THE TOOLS FOR
GREATNESS, STREWN SO CLOSE TO THESE
HERE DOORS, CARVED WITH THE DEFIANCE
OF OLD

288.
THE BEAST SUBMITS TO HIS SWORD IN ITS
BELLY
RUMBLES LIKE THE MOUNTAINS AS WORLDS
SHIFT, POWER ENDS
VICTORY RUNS RED INTO THE GROUND
THE MAN COLLAPSES, HIS OWN LIFE WANING
HIS LIFE'S WORK WAS NOT HIS OWN
SOMEWHERE, OUT THERE, A BOUNTY LIES
UNCLAIMED
NO ONE WILL KNOW
~~NO ONE WILL KNOW~~

289.

THE SKY IS BRUISED
I BAT AWAY INSECTS AND LET TODAY LAY TO
REST

290.

ARCTIC COLD RAGES AGAINST A BEACH OF
ASHES OF FIRES ONCE LIT, THE WARMTH
LONG SINCE LOST WITH THE AGES
ONE MAN ALONE AGAINST THE ROCKS
TEMPTS FATE AND RAGES AGAINST DICE
ONCE CAST
ONE MAN, NOW TWO, JOINED IN STUBBORN
DEFIANCE AND NAUGHT ELSE
A VILLAGE STANDING TALL, TEN SMALL FIRES
IN THE WIND

WE ARE ALL FULL OF BATTLECRIES

291.

I AM AT SEA AND IT RAGES AND IT SCREAMS
AND I SCREAM BACK AS WATER FILLS MY
THROAT AND I KNOW IT IS FUTILE, FOR THE
SEA IS STRONG AND I WILL NOT BE HEARD BY
IT, NOT EVEN ON THE CALMEST OF DAYS.

BUT THAT'S OKAY BECAUSE I AM NOT THE SEA
AND I CHOOSE TO HEAR MYSELF AND I HEAR
MY THOUGHTS AS I SHIVER AND I STAND ON
THE SAND AND I TASTE SALT ON MY LIPS LIKE
THE ASHES OF MY INNOCENCE. THERE WAS A
TIME, BEFORE TODAY, BEFORE I SAW THE
CRUELTY IN THE WAVES. TODAY I AM
CAUTIOUS. TOMORROW I WILL BE TOO.

I CHOOSE TO TOUCH THE SAND AND BUILD A
RAFT AND DO WHAT I ONCE DID BEFORE IN
DEFIANCE FOR I AM MY OWN PERSON AND
ONE, TWO, MORE STORMS CANNOT TAKE ME
FROM MY SELF. DEFIANCE IS QUIET AND I AM
NOT ALONE, BECAUSE ALTHOUGH I AM QUIET,
WE ARE QUIET TOGETHER.

WHEN THE SKIES ARE TRUE AND THE LAND'S
BELOW MY FEET I AM LUCKY, BECAUSE THERE
WAS A STORM BUT HERE I AM, BENEATH
THESE CLOUDS, AND THE WORLD IS MORE
GOLDEN THAN IT EVER WAS BEFORE THE
STORM. I AM SURE I AM SAFE BECAUSE YOUR
EYES ARE ON ME AND THEY ARE SO
BEAUTIFUL, AND I KNOW, SOMEHOW, THAT I

AMBER SELQET
CX

WE ARE ALL FULL OF BATTLECRIES

AM TOO, DESPITE ANGRY CUTS AND SALTED
LIPS. I AM BEAUTIFUL EVEN AS THE SEA IS
DARK AND MY RESOLVE GROWS WEAK
BECAUSE I AM STRONG BECAUSE I AM HERE. I
AM STRONG BECAUSE STRENGTH ISN'T
CONSTANT BUT NEITHER ARE THE SEAS.

I BUILD A SHIP AND I LEAVE SHAME IN THE
DUST. THE OCEANS DON'T GIVE A FUCK WHO
THE FUCK YOU ARE.

292.
AWAKENING BENEATH THE EMBERS OF
YESTERDAY
COLD AIR STINGS OPEN CUTS
THE WOUNDS HAVE NOT YET BRUISED
SHE LETS THE DAY MEET HER WOUNDS IN
DEFIANCE
LOOK AT HOW YOU HURT ME
WATCH ME AS I BLEED

AMBER SELQET
CXI

WE ARE ALL FULL OF BATTLECRIES

293.
CRY BABY, CRY FOR ME
CRY FOR US
CRY FOR TOMORROW WHEN WE WILL LIE,
ONCE AGAIN, IN THE DUST

294.
THERE'S LIONS IN THE DEN
LIONS, YES, BUT THERE'S LITTLE FIGHT LEFT
IN THEIR LIMBS

295.
I LOVE YOU, DARLING, AND I MISS YOU
BUT I'D PLUNGE THAT BLADE DEEPER IF I
GRIPPED ITS HILT AGAIN

296.
FORGIVE ME, MOTHER, FOR I HAVE TRUSTED
YOU ONCE MORE
PLEASE OVERLOOK THIS HERE
TRANSGRESSION

297.
INNOCENCE IS NOT A BLANKET ON WHICH ALL
OTHER SINS MAY LIE
LIFT THE VEIL, BLACK AND GREY
I SEE YOU FOR WHAT YOU ARE

298.
ALL WAS LOST IN THE NAME OF THE
TEMPTING PROMISES OF FAMILIAR BONDS
ALL WAS LOST AND WOUNDS WERE GAINED,
AND WE HAVEN'T LEARNT YET HOW TO HEAL

WE ARE ALL FULL OF BATTLECRIES

299.
ON IMPACT, MY WORLD HAEMORRHAGES THE
BRUISED COLOURS OF A BROODING SKY
SENSATION IMPLODES AND RENDERS ME
NUMB IN THE FACE OF SUNLIGHT
I AM A FOOL FOR NOBODY, BUT TONIGHT I AM A
FOOL FOR YOU
PERHAPS COLLISIONS ARE ACCIDENTAL AND
THESE PATHS WERE NEVER MEANT TO CROSS
MAYBE I AM SICK TO DEATH AND IT'S EASIER IF
YOU'RE STILL GOOD FOR ME
SWEET OPTIMISM PLACATES THE PAIN AS
TWILIGHT HITS

300.
TAKE WHAT THE FATES HAND YOU AND HACK
YOUR WAY TOWARDS THE SWEET UNKNOWN
MAKE THIS MOMENT YOUR WEAPON AND
CHOOSE HOW THE ARROW LANDS
DEFIANCE IS THE BATTLE CRY OF A
FRUSTRATED MAN
AND IT CONQUERS ALL DOUBTS BEFORE THEY
SOW

WE ARE ALL FULL OF BATTLECRIES

301.

CAN YOU FEEL MY DEFEATED HEART
REBELLING IN THE WIND?
WARM ME UP, SWEET ICARUS, HOLD MY
DREAMS CLOSE TO YOUR CHEST
FLY WITH ME UNDER THE WINTER SUN
BEYOND THIS WEARY PATH

302.

THE BANG OF MY CHEST IS THE DRUM OF OUR
DESTRUCTION AS I REBEL AGAINST YOUR
CAUSE
MY FINGERNAILS ARE UNDERLINED WITH
BLOOD AND IT IS MY OWN
I TAKE SOLACE IN DESTRUCTION AND CALL
DEFEAT A WIN
TOMORROW I WILL START TO REBUILD
AND IF IT SUCKS, I'LL START AGAIN

303.

COME HOME TO ME, SWEET OSIRIS
USURP THESE BLOODIED BONES
TAKE OUR SON UNDER YOUR WING
HE WILL AVENGE US YET

304.

BRAVE TALES OF WAR FROM THE PEN OF A
MAN WHO LIVES IN THE SHADE
FEAR OF JUDGEMENT, FEAR OF FEAR, GUIDE
THIS PEN AS HE PROOFS IT, ONCE, TWICE,
THRICE
A MAN WITHOUT CONVICTIONS WRITES THEM
INTO HIS PROSE
DESIRE FOR ACCEPTANCE COLOURS AND
HOLDS HIM BACK
PERHAPS HIS CHARACTERS WILL REMIND HIM
THAT TO LIVE IS TO CREATE WITHOUT FEAR
*EXPRESSION IS AT ITS TRUEST WHEN YOU
DON'T EDIT IT FOR ME*

305.

THE COLOUR OF THE WORLD MAKES HIS
SADNESS SEEM SILLY, SOMEHOW
AND THE DEAFENING LOUDNESS OF
LONELINESS REVERBERATES OFF HIS CHEST

"I AM ALONE"

THE MICE HEAR BUT THEY DO NOT MATTER,
AND SO ALONE HE STAYS

AMBER SELQET
CXVI

306.
FOOL ME ONCE, SHAME ON YOU
FOOL ME TWICE, SHAME ON YOU
FOOL ME, SHAME

307.
IT IS THE HEIGHT OF RIDICULOUSNESS, THAT
AFTER ALL THESE YEARS, ALL THESE BRUISED
VEINS, ALL THESE CUTS WHICH DO NOT HEAL
TWO SMALL WHITE PILLS HAVE CURED MY
ILLS
ABSURD

I LAUGH AT THE MOON UNTIL I AM CRYING AT
THE SUN, FROM A ROOFTOP IN SUBURBS
UNKNOWN
I'VE BEEN HURTING FOR SO LONG THAT IN ITS
ABSENCE IS A HOLE IN THE SHAPE OF
CONCERN
I AM UNSURE HOW I SHOULD FEEL

I SWALLOW MY PRIDE WITH MY PILLS AND
BEGIN ANOTHER DAY IN THE GREAT
UNKNOWN
THE RELIABLE LULL OF MY SADNESS IS GONE
AND I HAVE NOTHING BUT TIME
WHO AM I IN THE ABSENCE OF FEAR?

WE ARE ALL FULL OF BATTLECRIES

308.
NOVEMBER,
FRESH ANGER, TENDER ANGUISH
MY KNEES ARE SCRAPED AND IT'S NOT FROM
PRAYING
I THROW MYSELF AT THE CLIFF AND ROLL
DOWN THE HILL TO SICKLY SWEET
IGNORANCE

DECEMBER,
HANDS TOUCH HANDS
MY HEART IS A BROKEN BIRD AND I AM NOT
SURE THESE WINGS WILL FLY AGAIN
FORGIVE ME

APRIL,
I AM MADE OF BROKEN SHELLS
EACH MORNING WE FALL DEEPER INTO OUR
HEARTS
UNDER THE BEATING SUN WE HEAL
AGAIN, AGAIN, TOMORROW AGAIN

JULY,
THE SCARS ARE SLOWLY FADING
MY HEART DOES NOT HOLD BACK
WE STAND TOGETHER AT THE MOUNTAINTOP
AND DECLARE WHO WE ARE

DECEMBER,
FULL CIRCLE WITH NEW BLOOD IN OUR VEINS

AMBER SELQET
CXVIII

WE ARE ALL FULL OF BATTLECRIES

WE'VE BUILT A HEARTH WHICH NO LONGER
NEEDS TO HEAL
I AM YOURS AND YOU ARE MINE AND WE ARE
HOME

309.
A WOMAN UNDER A PALE OAK
UNDER THE LUNAR SKY
SHE SHAKES HER FIST AT THE GODS AND
DEMANDS PENANCE AS SHE COMMITS ACTS
WHICH HAVE NOT YET BEEN DECLARED SINS

310.
LOVE FEELS RELIGIOUS IF YOU DO IT RIGHT

311.
THE SHEEP SURROUND THE WOLF TODAY
UPRISING
JUSTICE
DEATH

312.
THE WORLD ISN'T HOW I PICTURED IT AND MY
STRENGTH ISN'T HOW I PICTURED IT
I THOUGHT I WOULD BE THORNS AND AXES
AND BLOOD IN THE SOIL
BUT INSTEAD IT IS THAT THE STRONGEST WAY
TO BE IS TO BE SOFT LIKE THE AFTERNOON
CLOUDS AND THE CARESS OF THE BREEZE
AND GENTLE FORGIVENESS
I AM ROSES AND DEFIANT KINDNESS IN SPITE
OF THE WORLD
BECAUSE OF THE WORLD

313.
WE ARE ALL OF US FLEDGLING GODS
GIFTED WITH THE CURSE OF DECISIONS

WE ARE ALL FULL OF BATTLECRIES

314.
YOU ARE THE SUNSET, EVERLASTING, EVER
CHANGING, EVER HERE, EVER THERE
YOU ARE THE SUNSET AND I FIND YOU IN THE
BLUES AND THE GREENS OF THE SEA AND
THE GOLD IN THE SAND AND THE RED IN MY
CHEEKS
YOU ARE THE SUNSET AND I LOOK FOR YOU IN
THE WARMTH OF EACH BREAKING DAY

315.
THE PEAKS OF THE LANDSCAPE ARE RUGGED
PILLARS TO FREEDOM
THE YEARS HAVE WORN THE STONE SMOOTH
NOT ONE FOOTHOLD REMAINS

316.
I THROW MY CAUTION AWAY

IT RETURNS

AMBER SELQET
CXXI

WE ARE ALL FULL OF BATTLECRIES

317.
I DON'T WANT THE COMFORT OF MONOTONY.

I WANT ALL THE SIN OF LIFE AND THE
FREEDOM OF DANGER. I WANT TO DRINK THE
PASSION OF OUR JEALOUSY AND CONSUME
YOU, AS YOU, TOO, CONSUME ME. I AM
GLUTTONY AND YOU ARE THE ALL THE
SWEETNESS OF THE WORLD AS YOU DRIP
DOWN MY THROAT, DOWN MY CHEST, DOWN.

318.
WE MEET WHERE THE LIGHT BURNS ETERNAL

319.
THE OLD GODS REMAIN
BUT EVEN THEIR HOPE WAVERS

WE ARE ALL FULL OF BATTLECRIES

320.
LIGHTER IN HER FINGERS, FIRE ON HER LIPS
BORNE OF BLOOD AND LIES, SHE CLAIMS
LIMBS, VOICES, LIVES
RED LAKES, JAGGED MOUTH

"I AM A YOUNG GOD
GIVE ME WHAT I AM OWED"

321.
LOVE-DRENCHED WORDS
PISTOLS DRAWN
HE AVENGES HER WITH HIS DYING BREATH
NEXT, HIS MOTHER MAKES THE SAME VOW

322.
JUSTICE CLOAKS HIM AS HE SEEKS MALICE
OUT FROM THE SHADOWS
HE'S SHINY AND NEW AND BUILT OF IRON AND
IDEALS
HIS FISTS MEET THE FLESH OF A LESSER MAN
BUT AT THE FINAL SECOND HE PULLS BACK
TONIGHT HE PROVES THAT HE IS DIFFERENT,
THAT HIS BRAND OF JUSTICE KNOWS NO END

MERCY IS FOR THE WEAK AND THE CAPTIVE
MAKES AN INEVITABLE ESCAPE
COMMITMENT TO A CAUSE REQUIRES THAT
YOU FOLLOW THROUGH
PRIDE ALONE DOES NOT TRAVEL ON THE
WIND

323.
THE URGE TO FEEL ALIVE GUIDES THEM TO
THE MOUNTAIN

"WHAT NOW?"
"WHAT THEN?"

WE ARE ALL FULL OF BATTLECRIES

324.
MORE WOLF THAN WOMAN,
SHE IS UNAPOLOGETICALLY FIERCE AND
DRIPS WITH PASSION
BUT WOLVES HAVE SHARP EDGES,
AND SHE WON'T APOLOGISE FOR SCARS LEFT,
EITHER

325.
MILK AND HONEYDEW IN A TEACUP
MY THROAT IS COATED WITH HUMBLE TRUTHS
'TIL DEATH DO US PART

326.
I JOURNEY TO THE MOON AND BACK AND FIND
I LOVE YOU STRONGER

327.
NOTHING IS BLUE TODAY

AMBER SELQET
CXXV

328.
YOU SHARPEN YOUR CLAWS WITHOUT ANY
INTENTION OF DIRTYING THEM
FALSE SECURITY IN EMPTY ACTIONS

329.
THE WALLS OF OUR BEING ARE ANCIENT
WALLS
PRIMED WITH THE BLACK MORALS OF OUR
FOUNDING FATHERS
LAYER UPON LAYER OF PRESENT OBSCURES
THE PAST, UNTIL WE NO LONGER REMEMBER
WHERE WE BEGAN, AND THE TIME TO TURN
BACK HAS LONG SINCE PASSED

330.
PICK A SIN AND LET IT DEVOUR THE
EMPTINESS INSIDE

WE ARE ALL FULL OF BATTLECRIES

331.
PRAY TO THE FOREST RUNNING WITHIN YOU
DEMAND IT RUN WILDER STILL AND FREE YOU
FROM THE SHACKLES OF STRAIGHT EDGES
BECOME A MONUMENT TO ALL THAT IS LIFE
AND BREED CONTEMPT INTO THE WORLD
WASTED OPPORTUNITIES ARE
UNACCEPTABLE
LET THE DEATH OF ALL THAT YOU ONCE WERE
BREATHE POTENTIAL INTO THE WORLD

332.
"DON'T PULL THE TRIGGER."

"SORRY."

KALEIDOSCOPE OF SOUR MEMORIES
CONTROL OVER THE GUN WAS A
COMFORTING LIE

333.
UNWAVERING IN WITCHING WAYS, SHE
SUCCUMBS TO THE PLEASURES OF SWEET
NOTHINGS AND WISHES OLD TERRORS AWAY

AMBER SELQET
CXXVII

334.
"DEATH IS A FACT OF THE UNIVERSE.
MEMORIES, RELATIONSHIPS, ROSES, THEY
ALL SHALL END. MAYBE YOU CAN DRAW IT
OUT. MAYBE YOU CAN'T. BUT THE BLOOMS
ARE HERE NOW AND SO ARE YOU, IF YOU
CHOOSE TO BE."

335.
SECOND TIME AROUND THE WHEEL
IT FEELS THE SAME
IT PULLS THE SAME
IT HURTS THE SAME

WE ARE ALL FULL OF BATTLECRIES

336.
FULL DISCLOSURE, UPFRONT HARSH TRUTHS.

"IF I LET YOU IN, YOU'RE IN, YOU CAN'T
LEAVE."

"PLEASE LET ME IN."

I LONG FOR A PROTECTED HEART ONCE
MORE
YOU CAN HELP AND, ONCE AGAIN, YOU DON'T
OFFER TO

337.
CANDLE FOR A BROKEN HEART
RED WAX PROMISES FREEDOM IN THE FORM
OF LUST

338.
ANGER AND FRUSTRATION SHAPE HIS HANDS
INTO DAGGERS AND HIS DEVOTION
DESTROYS HER SKIN

"AGAIN, PLEASE"

339.
PANDORA [PAN-DOHR-*UH*]
NOUN.

a. SHE SEEKS OUT THE UNKNOWN AND
    ALLOWS HER CURIOSITY TO CONSUME
    HER. SHE IS THE PROTECTOR OF
    GOODNESS AND SEEKS KNOWLEDGE
    ABOVE ORDER. HER INNOCENCE SPELLS
    DOWNFALL AND HER SINS SPELL TRUST
    ISSUES.

b. THE FIRST WOMAN. ALL THAT IS AND WILL
    BE FEMININE AND BEAUTIFUL AND
    TESTING. GENTLE AND FERTILE, LIKE
    DAMP SOIL AFTER SUMMER RAIN. SHE
    LOVES SUNFLOWERS AND THE SMELL OF
    OLD BOOKS.

c. I GAVE HER THE WORLD AND SHE
    RESPONDED IN KIND.

d. A PUNCHLINE ANTICIPATED BY THE GODS.

340.
"THE WAR SAVED OUR FAMILY.

WE THOUGHT HE WAS LOST. WE WERE SURE
OF IT. AND HE IS. WE ARE FREED."

341.
I'VE BEEN SEARCHING FOR BEAUTY FOR SO
LONG,
AND NOW I KISS YOUR NECK, YOUR ARMS,
YOUR LEGS, IN SEARCH OF HIDDEN RIVERS
AND OH
AND OH
HERE I GO AGAIN, LOST BETWEEN THE CURLS
OF YOUR HAIR AND THE CURVE OF YOUR LIPS
SO LONG, GOODBYE, GENTLE SANITY
YOU WERE SO OVERRATED, ANYWAY

WE ARE ALL FULL OF BATTLECRIES

342.
I DEFY YOU WITH ACCEPTANCE
NO SWORDS, NO WINS
BRING YOUR WRATH UPON ME FOR I FEEL IT
NOT
THE HEAT OF YOUR INTENTIONS IS SHALLOW
I WILL NOT REWARD YOU WITH BARED TEETH
THE FIGHT INSIDE ME IS RESERVED FOR
BATTLES WORTH BLEEDING OVER

343.
SIREN CALL OF A SLOW EMBRACE
TAKE ME INTO THE SHELTER OF YOUR HOME
FEED ME, LOVE ME, DANCE WITH ME IN THE
RAIN
YOUR FINGERS ARE TENDRILS AROUND MY
BEATING WINGS
WE ARE ONE AND WE ARE TWO
AND WHEN MY WINGS BEAT AGAIN I FIND
THEM CHAINED
UNTIL I BEGIN TO WONDER
PERHAPS THEY WERE ALWAYS SO?

WE ARE ALL FULL OF BATTLECRIES

344.
SIRE TO A LINE OF ONE
THE EGGS ALL BRE AK

345.
"YOUR BEST IS GOOD ENOUGH."

346.
BANG BANG
HE SHOOTS ME DEAD
AND RIPS HIS OWN SOUL APART

WE ARE ALL FULL OF BATTLECRIES

347.
HIS DELICATE FINGERS WAX PASSION ACROSS
THE SHEETS
AND COAX OUT CLUMSY WORDS AND
SHAMEFUL TRUTHS FROM DORMANCY
THERE IS SOMETHING ABOUT THE BRUSH OF
FINGERTIPS, SOME MUSIC IN THE AIR
AS THE HOURS WANE AND THE CANDLE WAX
FINDS A NEW HOME DRIPPING DOWN MY SKIN
HE KISSES ME AND CALLS IT AN ODE TO OUR
FUTURE
AND I FIND RELIEF IN SALTWATER TEARS
KEEP ME CLOSE IN YOUR HEART
MAY ALL LOST SOULS BE FOUND

348.
THE AIR IS COLDEST CLOSEST TO YOUR
WINGS
IN THIS LAND OF ENDLESS WINTER
YOU'LL FIND A WAY TO MAKE IT COLDER STILL

WE ARE ALL FULL OF BATTLECRIES

349.
I AM AN ARCHITECT OF YOUR DESPAIR
A BALLAD TO TEMPTING PROMISES, BETTER
LEFT UNSAID
AND YET, STILL SAID
YOU SHOULD HAVE KNOWN BETTER
YOU ARE FILTH AND YOU SULLY MY HEARTH
YOU ARE AN AILMENT ON THIS EARTH
AND I DON'T KNOW WHAT THE PURPOSE OF
LIFE IS
BUT IS SURE AS HELL ISN'T ENTERTAINING
YOU, A VIOLATION OF THE NATURAL ORDER

THE WHISPERS IN MY HEAD RESONATE
LOUDER WITH EACH PUNCH THAT CONNECTS
I WILL THEM TO LET ME LAY MY HEAD TO REST
BUT THEY WILL NOT BE EASILY WON
AND THEY GUIDE MY KNUCKLES PAST WHAT
WAS ONCE A COMFORTABLE EDGE

I AM THE FIRST CHALLENGER
AND TODAY I KNOCK LOOSE YOUR PRIDE

WE ARE ALL FULL OF BATTLECRIES

350.
A SHEEP IN A HERD OF WOLVES
A WOLF IN A PACK OF SHEEP
I AM BRAVE BECAUSE I HAVE TO BE

351.
SOFT SKIN AND BLEEDING GUMS,
TAINTED WORDS AND STAINED LIPS,
HIS FACE IS THE STUFF OF HYMNS.
CHUNKS OF MEAT BENEATH CRACKED NAILS,
SECRETS BEHIND THE CUPBOARD DOOR,
BUT FUCK, THE HEARTH LOOKS WARM.

DARK SCALES AND TENDED PLANTS,
SCARRED LEGS AND GENTLE WINDS,
HE IS A VISION OF THE DARK.
SWEET WORDS AND LOVING ARMS,
A VIVID LIFE, A PLACE TO REST,
HIDDEN BEHIND DUSTY, MARBLED THORNS.

WHAT MAKES A MONSTER? WHAT MAKES A
MAN?
BLOOD COURTESY OF THE "INNOCENT"

AMBER SELQET
CXXXVI

352.

I SCREAM AT THE DARKNESS AND IT SCREAMS
BACK
"I THOUGHT I WAS ALONE" I SAY
"I THOUGHT I WAS ALONE" IT SAYS

353.

POSSESSION OF DESIRE LEADS MY CLOUDED
MIND DOWN A TREACHEROUS PATH
I TRUST MY BROKEN HEART AS IT LEADS ME
ASTRAY ONCE MORE

354.

REALITY PUNCHES THEM IN THE GUT AND
STILL THEY RAIN DEFIANCE ACROSS THE
BATTLEFIELD
THE FATES ARE NOT OFT WRONG
BUT PERHAPS THAT IS BECAUSE THEY ARE
NOT OFT CHALLENGED

355.
HER FACE IS A MESS OF GASHES AND ANGRY
WOUNDS
IT IS QUIETER NOW
I DO NOT TELL HER SHE IS MORE BEAUTIFUL
NOW
IT WOULD BE AN INSULT
FORCED GROWTH IS THE UGLIEST REALITY
OF THEM ALL

356.
I AM THE LAST OF A TRIBE OF ONE
AND I BID MY TRADITIONS GOODBYE FOR A
SINGLE TEMPTING PROMISE

WE ARE ALL FULL OF BATTLECRIES

357.
SIBERIA, 1922
IT HAS BEEN MANY A MOON SINCE
FOOTSTEPS AND PLANTED FLAGS
THE ETERNITY OF NOTHING IS RAVENOUS,
AGGRESSIVE, RESOLUTE
THE WAITING HAS LONG SINCE TURNED TO
HOPING, TO ACCEPTING, "THIS IS THE WAY
THINGS HAVE ALWAYS BEEN"
THE GODS ARE SO OLD THAT THEY FORGET
THEIR OWN NAMES
TEARS HERE ARE ETERNAL, IMMORTAL
CAST IN ICE
NOBODY REMEMBERS WHO, WE CALL HIM THE
FIRST MAN
HE BUILT A WALL OF SADNESS
ONE WALL, NO DOOR
AND THEN SHE ARRIVES, <u>WITH A HATCHET</u>

358.
WOVEN WIND AROUND MY ANKLES
MY HAIR IS SWEPT WILD BUT MY THOUGHTS
REMAIN STILL

AMBER SELQET
CXXXIX

WE ARE ALL FULL OF BATTLECRIES

359.
YOU ARE THE BRAVEST
THE MOST NOBLE OF WARRIORS
TO LASH OUT AT THE WEAKENED AMONG US
TAKE OUT YOUR INADEQUACIES ON THE
WEAK, TO BLAME IT ON THE STARS
THIS WORLD HAS FORGOTTEN TO TEACH YOU
THE LESSONS IT FORCE FED ME

MY VISION HAS NOT YET FAILED ME AND STILL
I CANNOT FIND ONE VAGUELY REDEEMING
QUALITY TO JUSTIFY SUCH A WASTE OF TIME
AS TO SPEND ANOTHER GODFORSAKEN
MINUTE THINKING OF YOU

360.
THEN ZEUS HELD YOU IN HIS ARMS
WHAT A TERRIBLE WASTE OF TIME

AMBER SELQET
CXL

361.
I HAVE FALLEN HEAD OVER HEELS IN LOVE
WITH THE NOTION OF BEING ALIVE, *TRULY
ALIVE*, IN THE WAY THAT SONNETS *DEMAND*
MY HEART THRUMS WITH A THOUSAND
FIREFLIES, AND THEY KEEP MY NERVES
INCENSED
I FEEL SPARKS AND TWITCHES IN MY FINGERS
AS A MELODY SETS THE AMBIENCE
I HEAR THE RUSH OF THE BREEZE, THE
SUGAR OF THE BIRDS, THE SLURP OF MY
COFFEE UP A STRAW
OH, IT'S TRUE, IT'S A WONDERFUL WORLD
AND IT'S ALL THE MORE LOVELY FOR YOU

362.
MY GREEDY HEART HAS FALLEN IN LOVE WITH
YOU TOO MANY TIMES

WE ARE ALL FULL OF BATTLECRIES

363.
THE BATTLES HAVE MELDED INTO ONE AND
THE SAME
HIS HANDS BLISTER WHERE THEY GRIP HIS
SPEAR
IN THE END, NOT WAR, BUT LUST DEFEATS
THE SAMURAI
IT IS THE INTOXICATING ALLURE OF SKIN
WHICH DRAWS HIM IN
DESIRE IN HAND, HE FOLLOWS THE SCARLET
ROSE PETALS, ABANDONED ON THE GROUND
A DISGUISE KISSES HIM AT THE DOOR, AND
WRAPS HIM IN A SILK SHEET AS HE STARES AT
HER LOVELINESS
HIS HEART BEATS FAST, AND A TEAR ROLLS
DOWN HIS CHEEK
HE KNOWS HIS MAKER IS NEAR
SHE FASTENS HIM TIGHTER WITH A SINGLE
VENOMOUS KISS
HE IS PALE LIKE THE SILK SHE WEAVES
HE IS DYING
"THANK YOU, GOODBYE"

WE ARE ALL FULL OF BATTLECRIES

364.
MY SADISTIC HEART MUSES ON US
I TAKE A SLEDGEHAMMER TO MY CHEST AND
FREE MYSELF OF A LIFETIME OF "NOT
ENOUGH"
I ACHE WITH THE SADNESS OF WINTER TREES
EVERYTHING TASTES LIKE BROKEN GLASS
MY LIPS DO NOT BLEED SO I CRY SOME MORE

365.
CAPTURED RAIN PARTS WAYS AND THE FIRST
RAYS OF FOREVER TWINKLE THROUGH
THE ROOTS OF THE ROSES THAT YEAR RAN
DEEP, WEDGED BETWEEN CRUMBLING ROCKS
STILL THEY HOLD FAST
STILL THEY BLOOM

366.
WE DIDN'T START THE FIRE
AND SO, WE LET IT BURN

AMBER SELQET
CXLIII

WE ARE ALL FULL OF BATTLECRIES

367.
THE LIGHT RISES AND ROMANTIC NOSTALGIA
LOSES ITS COLOUR
IN THE DAYLIGHT THE PASSION IS BRUISES
AND OUR MORALS ARE WORN

368.
THERE ARE TWO TITANS INSIDE YOU
ONE LUSTS FOR POWER
THE OTHER PINES FOR LUST

369.
YOU CALL MY NAME AND MY VEINS BURN LIKE
WHISKY
SELF CONTROL SURRENDERS TO THE HEAT

AMBER SELQET
CXLIV

WE ARE ALL FULL OF BATTLECRIES

370.

MY MIND IS EMPTY AS THE FAN HUMS LIKE A
SUNDAY
YELLOW HITS THE CEILING AND THE STARS
ARE LOST
I STARE THROUGH TEMPERED GLASS AND
SMELL MORNING DEW
YOUR ARMS CALL ME, PLEASE RETURN, AND
MY LIMBS ARE LOST BETWEEN FRESH
COTTON

371.

LET US BE FOREVER STRANGERS ONCE
MORE

372.

I SUBMIT TO MYSELF AND AM BECOME WHOLE

WE ARE ALL FULL OF BATTLECRIES

373.
AND I WATCH YOUR CHEST RISE AND FALL AS
THE FALSE EMPIRE I ONCE CHERISHED
CRUMBLES
THE SKIES ARE CLEAR AND THE SUNRISE
BRIGHT WITH UNCHAINED POSSIBILITY
I WILL HOLD YOUR HAND AND WE WILL
WANDER WITHOUT MAPS

374.
SUCCUBUS IN PLAIN DAYLIGHT
I STRAIGHTEN MY SKIRT AND RUN MY
FINGERS WHERE MY DESIRES DRIP SWEET
LUST DOWN MY LEG
I GIVE IN, LIKE I ALWAYS DO, AND MY MOUTH
WRAPS AROUND YOUR NAME

375.
IT IS IMPOSSIBLE TO PLEASE THE SAVAGE
TEMPTATIONS OF MY MIND, WITHOUT MY MIND
ITSELF CHANGING

WE ARE ALL FULL OF BATTLECRIES

376.
I LOOK OUT OF MY HELMET AND SEE THE
STARS EXPLODE

IT IS THE END OF THE WORLD AND I AM MORE
TERRIFIED THAN EVER OF ITS BEAUTY
IT SHOULD NOT LOOK SO

AND YET IT DOES
IN DEFIANCE, IT DOES

377.
HE USES HER AND SHE SAYS "THANK YOU"
HE TAKES HER ONCE AGAIN

378.
THE WAVES OF YOUR WORDS DON'T REACH
ME
WHITE NOISE FROM YOUR MOUTH
WE HAVEN'T TALKED IN MONTHS NOW
HELLO, GOODBYE, MY HEART BEATS ALONE

AMBER SELQET
CXLVII

379.
IN SEARCH OF SWEET NOTHINGS I EASE OPEN
YOUR CHEST, AND IT CREAKS LIKE A CASKET
THE TOMB THAT DOES NOT LOOK LIKE A TOMB
SMELLS LIKE MELANCHOLY AND REMINDS ME
LIFE CAN NEVER AGAIN BE THE SAME

I SIT BY MY BEDSIDE AND WEEP TEARS OF
FUTILITY

380.
HE APPEARS QUICKLY LIKE ROT ON A VINE,
AND COMMANDS WHAT IS LEFT OF MY
ATTENTION
TODAY I WASTE AWAY TO THE SOUND OF A
NEW PURPOSE

381.
THE FIRST TRIAL IS SURVIVAL
THE SECOND IS TO FIND THE THIRD

WE ARE ALL FULL OF BATTLECRIES

382.

CHERRY BLOSSOMS RAID SILK SKIN WITH
EACH OF HER SIMPLE KINDNESSES

THE YEARS FLY BY AS SHE SOWS SEEDS AND
PRUNES WEEDS AND STILL THE BLOSSOMS
BLOOM

I HAVEN'T SEEN HER IN A WHILE AND SO I SET
ON MY PATH ALONE

I FIND HER, ROOTS SET BY THE LAKE,
BLOOMING STILL

SHE HAS GIVEN HERSELF AWAY

AND LEAVES LOVELINESS IN HER WAKE

WE ARE ALL FULL OF BATTLECRIES

383.
WE STAND IN THE AIRPORT TOGETHER, LOST,
ALONE
NOT ONE OF US KNOWS WHERE WE ARE
HEADED
WHEN WE GAZE OUT WE SEE POSSIBILITY
BUT WE ALSO SEE RUNWAYS, ORGANISED
SUCCESS, THE END OF OUR JOURNEY

I, MYSELF, HAVE JUST ARRIVED
AND I'M NOT READY TO LEAVE YOU JUST YET

I WANDER THROUGH THE GIFT SHOP ONE
MORE TIME AND BUY THE KEY TO A LOCK
WHICH DOES NOT YET EXIST

384.
CRISP WHITE BEDSHEETS MOCK MY TRUE
DESIRES

AMBER SELQET
CL

385.
THE HUM OF THE ENGINE IS THE ONLY
REMINDER OF THE CAR.

"YOU PROMISED TO LOVE ME."
I LOOK TO MY SIDE AND SEE REGRET STARING
BACK AT ME. REGRET LOOKS ENTICING, BUT
SO DO NEW MISTAKES.

"I'M SORRY, I'M SORRY, I'M SORRY."
I PICKED A TERRIBLE TIME TO DO THIS. EACH
MILE STRETCHES LONGER STILL, AND MOSTLY
I AM SORRY THAT I CHOSE TO DO THIS RIGHT
NOW.

386.
ROSEBUDS IN A BATHTUB
I PUSH THEM TO THE SIDE AND DEVOUR HER

WE ARE ALL FULL OF BATTLECRIES

387.
THE OUTLINE OF HIS WORDS LOOKS BLURRY
IF I SQUINT I CAN SEE HALF TRUTHS
IF

I DO NOT SQUINT THIS TIME

388.
THE FOG OF AN AFTERNOON RUNS DOWN THE
WINDOWS, LIKE A RIVER OF OUR SINS
MELTED WAX FINDS THE DARKEST PARTS OF
YOU
AND I FIND NEW POOLS IN WHICH I MAY
WORSHIP YOUR WETNESS
MORE LUST STILL RUNS FROM YOUR LEGS
AND YOUR LIPS AND YOUR EYES
YOU BEG FOR MY DAMNATION AND I AM DUTY-
BOUND TO OBEY

WE ARE ALL FULL OF BATTLECRIES

389.
I LOOK INTO GLOWING EYES AND THE HARSH
REALITY OF JAGGED TEETH.

"YOU DO NOT BELONG HERE."

I WISH I COULD AGREE BUT I HAVE BEEN
THERE AND IT WAS NO BETTER THAN HERE. I
CLOSE MY EYES AND WISH THEY WERE OPEN.
I OPEN MY EYES AGAIN AND THE PATH IS
SCRATCHED INTO THE SKIN OF THE
WRONGED.

I HOLD TIGHT MY ARM TO STOP THE BLEEDING
AND TAKE MY LEAVE.

390.
THE CERTAINTY OF GOODBYE QUIETENS MY
HEART
I EXHALE RESTLESSNESS AND STALE AIR
YOU WILL ONLY BE MISSED BY THE MALLET IN
MY HAND

391.
THE FLAMES OF HIS TORMENT GREET ME AS I
TAKE HIM IN TO MY ARMS

392.
HIS ADVERTISED SINS ARE ANKLE DEEP
I EMERGE BATHED IN THE TREACLE OF RAW
HELLS
HE REACHES OUT FOR MY FINGERS AND I
SAMPLE HIS ROMANTICISED BOREDOM
THE STING OF THE ACID BEARS MY TEETH
FOR ME
A LACK OF SUBSTANCE LEAVES MY STOMACH
GROWLING AND SO THE WILD HUNT
CONTINUES

AMBER SELQET
CLIV

WE ARE ALL FULL OF BATTLECRIES

393.
AFFLICTIONS WHICH START AND END IN MY
MIND DISCERN LOVE AND HATE AND TREAT
THEM ALL THE SAME
I ALLOW TRIFLES AND REVELATIONS TO
CONSUME ME
ART SUBDUES THE VILLAINS OF MY STORY
AND MY PALETTE IS STAINED WITH
WISTFULNESS
AND THEN IT STOPS

.

AND IT STARTS ONCE MORE

394.
MISPLACED DESIRE LEAVES ME BEGGING FOR
YOU
YOU LEAVE ME HIGH AND DRY
I BOW TO YOUR MOST SELFISH WHIMS

AMBER SELQET
CLV

WE ARE ALL FULL OF BATTLECRIES

395.
FROM THE RIVERBANK THE STREAM LOOKS
GENTLER STILL
THERESA AN AFTERNOON BREEZE, AND THE
WORLD SMELLS LIKE HONEY
I WATCH MYSELF GO BY AND RECOGNISE
NOTHING
RAYS OF SUNLIGHT SPLINTER MAGIC ACROSS
OUT SKIN
I ROLL OVER AND TURN MY THOUGHTS TO
PATHS UNDECIDED

WE ARE ALL FULL OF BATTLECRIES

396.
THE WARMTH OF YOUR WORDS WRAPS
AROUND MY TONGUE AS YOU REACH OUT AND
URGE,

"ARE YOU READY TO TALK?"

YOU MAKE SHARING SEEM MAGICAL,
SOMEHOW.

AND, JUST FOR A MINUTE, THE REST OF THE
WORLD CAN HANG, BECAUSE JUST FOR A
MINUTE I FEEL THE PULL AT MY EDGES AS
THOUGHTS OF THE PAST BUBBLE UP, SHAPED
LIKE MESSY WORDS AND WET FACES.

I SHARE LIKE A STORM ALREADY BREWED,
BECAUSE IT HAS, AND I AM, AND IT'S LONG
BOILED OVER.

WE ARE ALL FULL OF BATTLECRIES

397.
*THE NUMBNESS OVERRIDE RENDERS THE
WORLD QUIETER*
FOOTSTEPS - NOW AIMLESS - GUIDE A SHELL
OF BEING
<u>THIS IS NOT EXISTENCE</u>

I KISS HER WITH MY LIPS AND WILL HER TO
JUST BE
MY MUSCLES TIGHT WITH PASSION, SHE
REMAINS COLD TO THE TOUCH

SHE FINDS A METEOR IN A BED OF
PERIWINKLES AND INHALES VOLATILE
DECISIONS
SHE BREWS GENTLE KINDNESSES BETWEEN
FICKLE MOMENTS
SHE GIVES HERSELF COMPLETELY TO THE
MOON AND HOWLS IN THE NAME OF ALL THAT
WAS ONCE HOLY TO HER
SHE ETCHES ART INTO THE WALLS WHERE
THE LIGHT ONLY HITS WHEN THE ORBS ARE
HIGHEST
AND I PRAY FOR HER MORTAL SOUL

SHE IS FOUND IN THE KARMA OF HER OWN
MAKING, IN THE PASSION AND THE HEAT AND
THE SAD AND THE WEAK
HER CANVAS FEELS LIKE SORROW BUT, FUCK,
IS IT PICTURESQUE

AMBER SELQET
CLVIII

WE ARE ALL FULL OF BATTLECRIES

THERE ARE HIGHS AND LOWS AND A
KALEIDOSCOPE I CANNOT DO JUSTICE WITH
MY TEXT

I AM A FOOL AND SHE IS FOUND AND TRUE
CURES ARE FOR THE BOLD

398.
MY EMPTY STOMACH FEELS JUST LIKE HOME

399.
MY SHELF IS MISSING A TRINKET.

"THIS CHAIN IS MINE. I WILL RETURN IT WHEN
THE TRADE IS COMPLETE."

I DON'T AGREE BUT THE VOICE IS GONE AND I
GO TO SLEEP AND HOPE I'LL WAKE UP WITH A
LITTLE MORE DIRECTION.

AMBER SELQET
CLIX

400.

I SEEK ETERNAL RELEASE IN THE FORM OF
DIRTY SHEETS AND DIRTIER THOUGHTS. I
ENVELOP MYSELF IN THE KNOWN AND FORGO
WONDERINGS OF FATE.

401.

MY HEART FEELS LIKE FIRST LOVE IN THE
PARK ON A THURSDAY AFTER SCHOOL; AND I
CANNOT BE TRUSTED TO KEEP MY COOL

402.

SHE SWINGS THE BLADE AND SCREAMS

"ARE YOU HAVING FUN?"

HE IS AT THE WRONG END OF THE BLADE AND
SHE KNOWS IT AND HE KNOWS IT AND THE
CROWS ON THE GATE AND THE WORMS IN
THE DIRT KNOW IT

PERHAPS HE NEEDS A BLADE OF HIS OWN

AMBER SELQET
CLX

403.
ONLY THE IMMORTAL CAN EVER REALLY DIE.

404.
THE DRAWN BLADE WHISPERS NOTHING FOR
CONVICTIONS ARE NOT YET WON
TODAY'S DESTRUCTION IS DEAFENINGLY
QUIET AS YOU BALL YOUR FISTS AND CURSE
NOTHING BECAUSE THE GODS WERE NEVER
LISTENING
YOU TELL YOURSELF YOU MADE A
DIFFERENCE AND CONTINUE DOWN A TRAIL
OF EMPTY REBELLION

405.
WISPS OF MADNESS TAUNT MY FINGERTIPS

I LAMENT MY LEAKING FREEDOM AND MY
SPIRIT DEEPENS IN SLUMBER

AMBER SELQET
CLXI

406.
HER WORDS ARE BOUND WITH LEATHER AND
AN UNTOUCHABLE BEAUTY WHICH ONLY
COMES WITH LONG WINTERS
I DON'T KNOW WHAT SHE'S SAYING BUT MY
THROAT HURTS ALL THE SAME
I CURSE THE COLD AND KEEP MY HANDS IN
MY GLOVES
SHE'S LONG LEARNT TO BUILD HER OWN
FIRES BUT MY ACTIONS TELL HER WHAT SHE
SOUGHT TO KNOW

407.
GREEDY GODS GUIDE GREEDIER ACTIONS
EMPTY VESSEL: SECURED
THESE HANDS DO THE WORK OF ME AND
MYSELF ALONE AS I CURSE THE OTHERS AND
CLAIM ETERNAL GLORY AS MY OWN

WE ARE ALL FULL OF BATTLECRIES

408.
I ENTER THE DIMENSION OF DREAMS AND
REPLACE NEW WORRIES WITH BLISSFUL
IGNORANCE
THESE ARE PROBLEMS FOR ME, FOR
ANOTHER TIME
AND WHEN I GLIMPSE A SHADOW THEY TAKE
ME BY SURPRISE
DÉJÀ VU

AMBER SELQET
CLXIII

409.
IT'S 5AM AND THERE'S ALREADY BLOOD UP TO
HER ELBOWS AS SHE LEANS OVER THE SINK
AND TRIES TO WASH AWAY HER POOR
CHARACTER
ITS NOT ENOUGH AND SHE DRAWS A BATH
BUT THE STEAM LACKS, SOMEHOW
SHE LAUGHS AT HER OWN INEFFECTUALITY
AS SHE RECOUNTS HER SIN TO AN AUDIENCE
OF ONE
SHE WILL ACCEPT HER FATE

IT'S MIDNIGHT AND SHE STANDS IN THE HALL,
OLD BLOOD UNDER HER NAILS, NEW BLOOD
ON HER TEETH
THE STING OF HER FIRST STRIKE NO LONGER
BITES, HER RECLAIMED REALITY IS HERS TO
KEEP
SHE IS NO SINNER; SHE IS A WARRIOR, A
MAIDEN, SLAVE TO THE FIGHT FOR JUSTICE
WHILE, SIX STEPS DOWN THE HALL, A LAMB'S
LIFE LEAKS BETWEEN THE FLOORBOARDS

THE FIRST SIN IS HONEST
THE SECOND NO LONGER SEEMS LIKE
SINNING AT ALL

WE ARE ALL FULL OF BATTLECRIES

410.
MY GUARDIAN ANGEL ARRIVES IN THE FORM
OF GUT FEELING
I TRUST MYSELF AND MOVE ON

411.
I FEEL I AM DESTINED FOR KINDNESS
AND SO I WRAP MY HANDS BEFORE I PUNCH
BECAUSE SOMETIMES VIOLENCE IS THE
ANSWER BUT MAYBE IT DOESN'T NEED TO BE
SO HARSH

412.
TEETH CUT IN TO FRESH PEACHES
SUGAR RUNS DOWN A CHIN
THE WORLD LOOKS GENTLE TODAY, A SKY OF
PASTEL PASSION

WE ARE ALL FULL OF BATTLECRIES

413.
ONE YEAR HAS PASSED AND I'M SURE I DID
NOT MEAN TO KNOW YOU SO WELL
I HAVE LONG FORGOTTEN MY OWN NAME

414.
OUR LIMBS TANGLE AND YOUR BREATH
DARKENS
YOU DO NOT LOVE ME
BUT PERHAPS YOU WOULD LOVE TO FUCK ME

415.
THERE IS TRUTH TO THE WINE

RESIDUAL WARMTH IN THE AIR AND CUPS IN
OUR HANDS
SHELTERED BETWEEN OLIVE BRANCHES
THIS NIGHT IS YOUNG BUT YOUR WORDS ARE
OLD
THE TARTNESS OF THE GRAPES DRAWS OUT
YOUR TRUTHS AND I LISTEN WHILE I STILL
CAN

AMBER SELQET
CLXVI

416.
NOT A MAN OF MANY WORDS
HE PULLS ME CLOSER
HS CHEST OPENS TO ME AND I STEAL A
GLANCE
HIS HEART SITS IN A FIELD OF LILACS, BY A
LAKE, ALONE

417.
HE IS WORRIED HE WILL NOT SUCCEED
AND SO IT IS HE SITS, AND WAITS
AND ACHIEVES EXACTLY NOTHING

418.
HUMMING FAM, MY THOUGHTS DRIFT AGAIN
TO YOU
I LIE IN A BED OF THE INEVITABLE AND LET
SUNLIGHT WARM MY SKIN

419.
TWO COMETS MEET LIKE DAGGER MEETS
KNIFE
SHARDS OF INADEQUACY RICOCHET
THROUGH THE UNIVERSE, A TESTAMENT TO
TWO STRONG WILLS, NEITHER STRONG
ENOUGH
THE SPRAY DOES NOT DISCRIMINATE
AND UNBEKNOWNST TO THE UNSULLIED
MASSES, THE INCOMING DESTRUCTION SHALL
LEVEL US ALL

420.
THE FURIES COME TO ME, SNARLING TEETH
AND SCREAMS CUTTING GASHES ACROSS MY
SKIN
ENOUGH- I FEEL THEIR DESPERATION LIKE
CLAWS IN MY CHEST, BORNE FROM THE
BLOOD OF 2AM MISTAKES
I CUT THEM FREE OF THEIR CHAINS AND WISH
THEM WELL AS THEY DESCEND
SOMETIMES GOOD PEOPLE MUST DO
TERRIBLE THINGS IN THE NAME OF FLEETING
MORALITY

AMBER SELQET
CLXVIII

WE ARE ALL FULL OF BATTLECRIES

421.

I LEAVE AGAIN WITH THE DYING MOON
WRAPPED IN FABRIC MEANT FOR ANOTHER
TIME
THE MISMATCH OF MY HEART LEAVES PINK
TRAILS ACROSS THE SKY

I TURN THE KEY AND ENTER MY OWN BLANK
PAGE AND WAIT TO BE CALLED UPON ONCE
MORE

422.

HE PLUNGES THE BLADE THROUGH MY
HEART; I FEEL THE WARMTH OF NOSTALGIA
LEAK INTO THE CARPET AS MY MOUTH FORMS
USELESS WORDS
HE DRIVES IT DOWN DEEPER STILL AND I BEG
FOR MY OWN DAMNATION; COME SOONER
PLEASE
THERE IS NO REST FOR THE WICKED, AND
HE'S WELL PAST GONE
I WEEP FOR MY OWN INNOCENCE AND WISH
ONCE AGAIN MY MOUTH HELD FANGS

WE ARE ALL FULL OF BATTLECRIES

423.
EMPTY BATTLEFIELD
BROKEN SWORDS
ONE HUNDRED MEN WHOSE SCARS WILL
RETURN HOME WITH THEM
ONE HUNDRED MORE WHOSE SCARS WILL
NOT

424.
I FIND YOU IN THE DUSK AND YOU TAKE ME
BETWEEN YOUR SHEETS
I SINK MY TEETH INTO YOU AND DRINK EVERY
LAST DROP OF YOU IN
YOU LEAVE YOUR MARK ON MY SKIN AND I
HOPE FOR NEW SCARS
IT DOESN'T HAVE TO LAST

WHEN THE MOONLIGHT REMINDS US WE ARE
LONELY AND THE SPACE BETWEEN MY LEGS
THROBS I MOAN OUT FOR YOU, ONCE MORE,
AGAIN
AND BETWEEN THE SWEAT AND THE SPIT OUR
SOULS LEAK OUT
AND THEN YOU RUIN ME ONCE MORE
IT DOESN'T HAVE TO LAST, *AND PERHAPS
THAT WHY IT DOES*

WE ARE ALL FULL OF BATTLECRIES

425.
YOU KISS ME LIKE AN OCEAN

"I RESPECT YOU"

YOU TAKE ME ON MY KNEES AND LEAVE ME IN
RUINS
YOU SHOVE YOUR FINGERS DOWN MY
THROAT AND CHOKE ME ON MY OWN LUST
I AM A PILE OF SEX AND HUNGRY MOANS, AND
I AM SURE THAT YOU REALLY DO

426.
THE SKIES ARE SINCERE AND THE AIR IS STILL
AND THIS MOMENT FEELS LIKE GENTLE
PASSION
THE SOIL IS FERTILE LIKE MY MIND AND I
ALLOW MY MIND TO WANDER AND I SMELL
FRESH CUT GRASS
THERE ARE STAINS ON MY KNEES BECAUSE I
AM ONE WITH THE EARTH AND I EXHALE
WARM INTENTIONS AS THE DANDELIONS
SCATTER

AMBER SELQET
CLXXI

WE ARE ALL FULL OF BATTLECRIES

427.
EVEN THE BLUEST SKY FADES TO BLACK
MY THOUGHTS ARE FRESHLY CLOAKED IN
DARKNESS AND THE TRUTH OF THE NIGHT
COAXES OUT THE SECRETS I KEEP FROM
MYSELF
IN THE SHADOWS I FEEL MY WAY TOWARDS A
NEW REALITY I HAVE BEEN AVOIDING
I WATCH THE CITY LIGHTS DIM AND GREET MY
NEWFOUND CLARITY WITH OPEN ARMS AND
CLOSED EYES
I TAKE MY NEW LEASE WITH ME INTO THE SUN
AND IT RINGS TRUER STILL

428.
I DON'T REMEMBER YOU
BUT YOU'RE THE FEELING I STILL GET WHEN
IT'S 2AM AND I CAN'T SLEEP, THERES TOO
MUCH LIGHT, AND I FEEL UNEASE CRAWLING
UP MY SPINE

429.
I WATCH MY SON TUMBLE FROM THE SKIES

AMBER SELQET
CLXXII

430.
UNWELCOME EMOTIONS OVERTAKE ME IN
THE FORM OF HIDDEN TEARS AND DEFEND
MYSELF WITH FISTS

431.
THE OLD GATE CREAKS LIKE BRITTLE BONES

THE STRANGER DECLARES WAR, AND HOLDS
A WEAPON HIGH
I CANNOT SEE IT CLEAR BUT THERE IS BLOOD
ON HIS FISTS

"NOW IS THE TIME FOR MAKING OLD ENEMIES"

HE CUTS INTO ME WITH GUILT AND
FORGOTTEN REGRETS

"NOW BEG"

I CRY FOR MY LOST INNOCENCE AND WISH I
KNEW THE NAME OF MY VILLAIN

432.
MY ARMS ACHE
I HAVE LONG FORGOTTEN WHAT IT IS I CARRY
BUT I BRING IT WITH ME ALL THE SAME

433.
CHOKE ME AND PULL MY HAIR
RUIN ME BEFORE YOU LEAVE ME
I AM GREED, HUNGER, SINFUL LUST AND I
LONG TO SWALLOW ALL THAT YOU GIVE
MY LIPS WRAP AROUND A POPSICLE AND I
KNOW IT ISN'T YOU

434.
I GIVE MYSELF COMPLETELY AND CONDEMN
FREE WILL TO THE GRAVE

435.
*SHE THOUGHT SHE WAS DONE WITH THE
SERPENT*

HER FINGERS ARE BLEEDING AND WEARY
FROM A LONG BATTLE NOT WON, YET NOT
LOST COMPLETELY EITHER
SHE DEFENDED HERSELF IN ONE WAY, IF NOT
ANOTHER
SHE WANDERS BETWEEN THE REEDS AND
THE SUGARY SCENT OF FREEDOM, BRUSHING
HER HANDS THROUGH NEW POSSIBILITIES
BUT THE WIND HAS CHANGED, AND SHE IS
NOT YET ESCAPED FROM THE GRASS
THE REEDS SMELL LIKE SHARPENED SCALES
AND ENDLESS TRAUMA
SHE PICKS UP HER LIFE AND *TAKES FLIGHT*

A COWARD ROCKS ON A CHAIR AND WATCHES
HER RUN AND WONDERS IF SHE WILL MAKE IT
BEFORE NIGHTFALL

AMBER SELQET
CLXXV

436.
3, 2, 1
I'VE BRACED FOR IMPACT AND BAD
OUTCOMES
I BREATHE IN SLOW MOTION AND MUSTY AIR
THE BLOW LANDS BESIDE MY HEAD AND I FIND
MYSELF THANKING MY ASSAILANT, BEGGING
FOR MORE

437.
I SHED MY OUTER SHELL AS I LIE BETWEEN
YOUR ARMS AND RELEASE MY BURDENS INTO
THE WORLD
YOU DON'T OFFER ADVICE, BUT I AM HEARD
WE DON'T MOVE BUT YOU'RE CLOSER
BREATHE IN, BREATHE OUT
I PURPOSEFULLY FORGET MY JACKET SO
THAT I MIGHT RETURN TO RETRIEVE IT

WE ARE ALL FULL OF BATTLECRIES

438.
THE ENERGY OF THE MOMENT OVERWHELMS
HIM AND HE STANDS ALONE ON THE
PAVEMENT
HE WATCHES SENSE KISSES HIM GOODBYE
THE OVERHEAD NEON FRAMES HIS GOOD
INTENTIONS BUT DOES NOT SOFTEN THE
STRIKE
I WATCH HIS EYES DIE AS HIS BREATHING
SLOWS AND I WEEP FOR HIS DEPARTING
VIRTUE
HE IS REBORN WITH A HATRED HE AIMS AT
LOVING LIPS AS HE DRIVES AWAY ANY HOPE
OF SOLACE
THE WORLD OWES HIM
AND I WATCH THE SCORNED HEARTS OF HIS
LABOUR MULTIPLY LIKE CRACKS IN THE
GLASS

439.
I MEET THE PALE REAPER ONCE AGAIN
HE WEEPS MORE THAN I REMEMBER
MY SOUL WEIGHS MORE THAN I WANT IT TO,
OR MAYBE I JUST THINK THAT BECAUSE I
KNOW I SHOULD
I WATCH THE UNIVERSE SIGH AS I WELCOME
THE BEGINNING OF THE END ONCE MORE

AMBER SELQET
CLXXVII

WE ARE ALL FULL OF BATTLECRIES

440.

I AM TRAPPED INSIDE MY OWN SKULL AND I
BEG FOR SWEET RELEASE

I FELL MYSELF ANGER AT THE ANNOYANCE OF
MY OWN DESPAIR, REPEATED ALOUD ONCE
MORE

BUT THESE ARE DESPERATE TIMES

AND SO THE DEVICE OF MY OWN TORMENT IS
MY OWN MIND

I FEEL THE GEARS TIGHTEN WITH EACH
MOMENT AS MY PATIENCE WEARS THINNER,
BUT MY MIND CANNOT STOP

I AM SURE SALVATION LIES WITH THE TEA
LEAVES BUT THE KETTLE IS TOO LOUD AND
TOO SLOW AND I HAVE NOT THE TOLERANCE
OF YESTERDAY

IT IS ALL TOO MUCH AND I AM ANGRY
BECAUSE THE WORLD DOES NOT KNOW AND
IT SHOULD

AND IN MY SOLO PURSUIT OF MENTAL
RELEASE THE SILENCE OF LONELINESS
WINDS ME

TODAY I AM DEFEATED

I YIELD TO SLUMBER AND PRAY TOMORROW I
FARE BETTER

BUT SAFETY IS A FARCE AND MY DREAMS ARE
ENVELOPED IN THERE MISTS OF FACELESS
FIENDS, AGAIN

AMBER SELQET
CLXXVIII

441.

HE SOWS THE SEEDS OF CHAOS WITHOUT
DISCRIMINATION

442.

HIS HUSHED WHISPERS DECLARES HE LOVES
HER OVER DIM LIGHTS AND TAKEAWAY MEALS
SHE MELTS INTO HIS ARMS AND HIS WORDS
ALIKE
SHE IS SURE OF HIM TODAY, TOMORROW, AND
IN TWO YEARS FROM NOW WHEN HE TAKES
THE KNEE
THE NEW YEAR BRINGS UNCOVERED
DECEPTION AND ANGRY TEARS
HE'S DECEIVED HER, OR MAYBE SHE
DECEIVED HERSELF

443.

I LIE ON THE BED OF VENUS IN SHEETS OF
WOMEN, STARLIGHT AND HONEY
MY MOUTH MOVES AND STUPIDITY ESCAPES
I HAVE TRADED MY MORALS AND BETTER
JUDGEMENT FOR TEMPORARY DISTRACTION
AND MY MIND HAS YET TO SWAY

WE ARE ALL FULL OF BATTLECRIES

444.
THE FRUSTRATION OF MY MIND BORES DEEP
INTO MY SKULL AND MY VERY EXISTENCE
SCREAMS FOR BLOOD
I AM MY OWN FRUSTRATION AND DEATH AND
LIFE AND INEXPLICABLE EMOTIONS
MY LIMBS ARE FASHIONED OF OLD STORIES
AND TORMENTS AND WISTFUL LOVE FOR
UNDERSTANDING
THERE ARE SENSATIONS IN MY LUNGS WHICH
LONG FOR RELEASE BUT I CAN'T FIND THE
MEANS TO SHARE
AND SO AS MY LUNGS DEFLATE, STILL I KNOW,
WITH EACH INHALATION THE SAME STALE AIR
WILL RETURN

445.
CRASS HUMOUR AND CONVERSATION TOPICS
SPICED WITH CANDID COMMENTS DISTRACT
FROM A REALITY OF HIDDEN PAIN, SHOVED
BACK INTO THE CORNER

446.
THE STEEL OF HIS INTENTIONS WEARS MY
NERVES
I AM WITH THE WIND
I AM TOO TIRED AND I HAVE FOUGHT TOO
MUCH FOR MORE POINTLESS CONFLICT
MY SKIN IS TOUGH BUT I HAVE HAD ENOUGH

447.
I THRASH AGAINST REALITY AND BREED MY
OWN RELIGION
I AM MY OWN GOD AND I WORSHIP MY OWN
BODY HENCEFORTH
LET ALL WHO TOUCH ME FEEL MY WRATH OR
FEEL MY LOVE
I AM JEALOUS OF INNOCENCE AND READY
FOR A FIGHT

448.
WE SHARE THE SAME BURDEN, SAME LIE
YOU CONDEMN ME TO STAND TRIAL ALONE

AMBER SELQET
CLXXXI

WE ARE ALL FULL OF BATTLECRIES

449.
EVERYTHING FUCKING HURTS SOMETIMES
IT BECOMES MY NEW NORM
AND MY OLD AVERAGE BECOMES MY NEW
IDEAL
A MAN HOLDS OPEN ONE DOOR AND I GIVE MY
MIND AWAY FOR THE TENTH TIME TODAY

450.
*SHE LOVES HER SO, AND SHE FORCES HER
TO KNOW*

451.
MY THROAT WEAKENS BETWEEN YOUR
FINGERTIPS
YOU WON'T LEAVE
MY VOICE IS DUST

452.
NIGHT LIGHTS DANCE ACROSS THE
WINDSHIELD
ONE HAND IS ON THE WHEEL AND THE OTHER
CLENCHES MY SINS
HYPNOTIC ECHOES AND ELECTRIC DRUMS
CONTRAST WITH A SLOW AND STEADY HEART
I AM COLD TO THE BONE AND LOOKING TO
GET LOST
I RUN AWAY AND FIND MYSELF WITH THE
RISING SUN

453.
THE BREAK IS NEVER CLEAN
EXPECTING IT TO BE WAS FOOLISH
<u>DO I CUT OFF MORE NOW OR RUN THE RISK
OF FESTERING?</u>

454.
YOU'RE ARTWORK
A FUCKING *MAGNUM OPUS*
FRAMED IN GOLD, YOU'RE MADE OF HUMBLE
PAPER AND GENTLE LINES
WHEN I LOOK CLOSE I SEE WHERE YOU
BROKE
A LITTLE TEAR
A LITTLE SCRATCH
A MARK ON YOUR SKIN
AND YET, WHEN I WALK AWAY I ALWAYS FIND
MY EYES RETURN
FOR YOU ARE BEAUTIFUL IN SPITE OF THE
WORLD YOU SEE
AND LIFE LOOKS A LOT MORE BEAUTIFUL ON
YOU THAN I EVER THOUGHT IT COULD

455.
SMALL THINGS FEEL LIKE BIG THINGS IF YOU
DO THEM RIGHT

456.
IT'S INEVITABLE LATELY, THAT I FIND
DISAPPOINTMENTS ALONGSIDE YOU

AMBER SELQET
CLXXXIV

WE ARE ALL FULL OF BATTLECRIES

457.
TALKING ABOUT THE WORLD IS NOT THE SAME
AS BEING ONE WITH IT
AND YOUR PRETENTIOUS WORDS WILL FOOL
ME NOT
I SEE YOU
AND I KNOW HOW *LITTLE* YOU HAVE LIVED

458.
I FIND SERENITY IN THE SHOWER
AND IRRATIONALITIES WASHES AWAY
IT BECOMES CLEARER TO ME WHICH WOES
WERE BASED IN FICTION

459.
IT WAS EASIER WHEN I DID NOT BLEED FOR
THE INJUSTICES OF THE WORLD
HERE I LIE, HAEMORRHAGING SLOWLY
I NOTICE A WARMTH IN THE THREAD OF MY
VEINS I DID NOT HAVE BEFORE

WE ARE ALL FULL OF BATTLECRIES

460.
I LOOK INSIDE YOUR SOUL AND FIND BROKEN
BONES RAISED SCARS
*AND SO I KISS YOU BENEATH THE MIDNIGHT
SKY*
YOU TASTE LIKE SHINY MORALS AND
FORGIVENESS AND INDISPUTABLE TRUTHS
AND RAMEN AND COFFEE AND TANGLED
LIMBS BETWEEN BEDSHEETS
MY HEART HAS BEEN HUNGRY FOR YOURS
AND FOR THE FIRST TIME IN A LONG TIME I AM
HOME

461.
I CAN BARELY BREATHE BETWEEN YOUR
SCREAMS
MUCH LESS HEAR MYSELF

462.
I GIVE YOU MYSELF FOR A SINGLE ROSE AND
FALL INTO YOUR ARMS

AMBER SELQET
CLXXXVI

WE ARE ALL FULL OF BATTLECRIES

463.

YOU WELCOME ME WITH AN OPEN HEART BUT
I CANNOT ENTER
HANDS AROUND YOUR HEARTH PUSH ME
AWAY
YOU SEE
YOU DO NOTHING
PERHAPS THIS IS TEMPORARY, PERHAPS NOT
TIME OR MY HEART, ONE WILL SURELY TELL

464.

THERE IS STRENGTH IN THE PLIGHT OF THE
PREY
INSTINCT GUIDES CLAWS BUT DESPERATION
WINS BATTLES
THE CRIES OF THE UNDERDOG GUIDE
HONEST STRUGGLES AND HARSH DECISIONS

465.

"YOU ARE NOT ALONE.
TOMORROW YOU WILL NOT BE ALONE
EITHER."

AMBER SELQET
CLXXXVII

466.
HE CANNOT BE TOUCHED BY DEATH. HE STILL
DOESN'T KNOW WHAT IT MEANS TO FEEL
ALIVE.

467.
I AM ALONE WITH MY THOUGHTS, BUT THEY
DO NOT SIMPLY TAUNT ME LIKE THEY ONCE
DID.

NOW THEY NIP AND BITE AT MY EXPOSED
FLESH, AND I CANNOT ESCAPE. I EXPERIENCE
EACH MOMENT AGAIN AND AGAIN, ENDLESSLY
HEALING, ENDLESSLY INJURED, AND LONG
FOR COMA ONCE MORE.

YOU DO NOT SEEK EXPLANATION FOR MY
MOOD AND I WISH YOU WOULD AS YOU ONCE
HAD. RED CLOUDS CAST ENDLESS DARK AND
FRAME MY TRUE REALITY. I WONDER IF YOU
WILL ASK ABOUT THE CLOUDS TOMORROW.

AMBER SELQET
CLXXXVIII

WE ARE ALL FULL OF BATTLECRIES

468.
YOU FEEL LIKE MIDNIGHT ON A TUESDAY
WHEN THE CLOUDS ARE GREY AND LAZY AND
THE SKY IS DARK AND THE MOON IS
NOWHERE TO BE FOUND
YOU FEEL LIKE WHEN THE CURTAINS CLOSE
AND THE MUSIC STOPS AND THE TRAIN IS
SCREECHES TO A HALT AT THE STATION
I FIND YOU IN THE THREAT OF YESTERDAY
AND THE REGRETS OF THE MORNING AND THE
SCARS ACROSS MY KNEES
YOU'RE THERE IN THE COLDEST CHILL OF THE
WINTER-TOO-SOON AND THE PRICK OF A
HIDDEN THORN
I HEAR YOU WHEN I KNOW YOU'RE NOT
THERE, IN THE DRIPPING TAP AND THE SIGH
OF THE DOOR

MY HEART BEATS STRONGER FOR THE SAKE
OF YOU, IN THE HOPES ADRENALINE WILL
PROTECT MY FREEDOM

I AM STUBBORN ENOUGH TO SURVIVE ONCE,
TWICE, HOWEVER MANY TIMES IT TAKES
UNTIL THE RED WINE CLOUDS MY MIND AND
ALLOWS ME ONCE AGAIN TO FUCKING REST

YOU'RE NOT HERE AND YOU'RE HURTING ME
AND I AM GODDAMN DONE

AMBER SELQET
CLXXXIX

WE ARE ALL FULL OF BATTLECRIES

469.
THERE IS STRENGTH IN SURRENDER
IN UNDERSTANDING WHEN THE CLOUDS
WON'T MOVE
BUT STANDING FIRM IN THE MUD ALONGSIDE
MORALS IN THE RAIN

470.
THERE IS COMFORT IN GENTLE MOMENTS:
1.   STEAM FROM THE KETTLE
2.   SOFT BLANKETS
3.   THE SOUND OF LAUGHTER FROM
     ANOTHER TABLE
4.   COMING HOME AND SEEING YOU

AMBER SELQET
CXC

471.

THERES A RUSTLING IN THE TREES AND THEY
WHISPER, *RUN*
ARMAGEDDON IS NIGH AND IT FEELS ALL TOO
FAMILIAR
I AM NOT SURE WHERE TO REST MY
FEATHERS BUT I CAN REMEMBER
EVERYTHING THAT EVER HAS BEEN AND I
CANNOT RECALL HOW IT WAS THAT WE CAME
TO BE HERE NOW
BUT I DO KNOW THAT THE WORLD HAS ENDED
TWICE BEFORE
I KNOW THAT WE'VE DONE IT BEFORE
I KNOW THAT WE'LL DO IT AGAIN
SURVIVAL IS A PRIMAL NEED AND IN THE FACE
OF DEVASTATION I WILL KNOW WHAT MUST BE
DONE
AND I TRUST THAT YOU WILL, TOO

472.

PERHAPS IT IS INEVITABLE
THAT I SLEEP A LITTLE DEEPER, A LITTLE
LONGER WHEN I LIE IN YOUR ARMS
FOR TOGETHER WE HAVE BUILT MANY
DREAMS
AND I INTEND TO SEE THEM THROUGH

AMBER SELQET
CXCI

473.
HE FALLS IN LOVE WITH HER DARKNESS
BECAUSE HE WANTS TO BE THE SUN
AND PULLS HER INTO HIS SELFISH ARMS
UNWILLING HER TO GROW

474.
THE UNVARNISHED REALITY OF THE MIRROR
PUTS YOUR SUGARED WORDS TO SHAME

475.
THE CUT STINGS BUT I AM WEARY FROM THE
ROAD
SO I LET MY ARMS HANG BY MY SIDE
AND MY TONGUE STAYS AT REST

476.
MY SOUL MEETS MY HEART AT THE TRAIN
STATION
IT'S LOUD AND INDELICATE AND MADE OF
STEEL AND PROSE
IT BEATS FOR YOU, PASSIONATELY,
DELIBERATELY, PURPOSEFULLY
AND WILL ALWAYS COME HOME TO YOU

477.
I AM PROTECTED BY THE KILL OF THE NIGHT
I PLACE THE SKULL OF THE OX OVER MY
SHOULDERS AND THANK THE FOREST FOR
THE MEAL
IT SMELLS LIKE IRON AS MY ARMS SWAY IN
THANKS
THERE IS A MADNESS BELOW THE SURFACE,
AND I FEEL IT GROW WITH EACH STEP
THE BLOOD MOON DRIPS WITH THE WISDOM
OF THE WOLVES AND I HEED THE CALL OF THE
HUNT

WE ARE ALL FULL OF BATTLECRIES

478.
I EMBRACE MOTHER NATURE AND SHE PULLS
ME INTO HER ARMS AND WE LOOK AT THE
FLOWERS IN THE TREES SO LONG THAT THEY
APPEAR IN MY HAIR AND BETWEEN MY
FINGERS

"IT HAS BEEN SO *LONG*, CHILD"

THE CRACK IN HER VOICE SOUNDS LIKE A
FALLING TREE AND I FEEL GUILT TIGHTEN MY
THROAT AND MY RESOLVE
I SIGH AN OLD SIGH, BECAUSE I KNOW
BETTER
AND AM GRATEFUL TO BE ONE AGAIN

WE ARE ALL FULL OF BATTLECRIES

479.
IT IS THE FIFTH DAY AND I RAKE THE GROUND
AND TEND THE LEAVES ONCE AGAIN
THERE IS PURPOSE IN MONOTONY AND I
ALLOW THE RHYTHMIC NATURE OF
REPETITION TO CARRY ME THROUGH THE
HOURS
SOMEWHERE BETWEEN THE DIRT AND THE
PHASES OF THE SUN I LOSE MY PURPOSE TO
THE HYPNOSIS OF HARD LABOUR

THE CROW ASKS ME WHAT MY GOALS ARE
AND AS MY WORDS CARRY THEIR MEANING
THEY FEEL CLOSER AGAIN, SOMEHOW

480.
"YOU DON'T NEED TO WAIT UNTIL TOMORROW
TO FORGIVE YOURSELF"
THE FRANKNESS OF THE WALLS BRINGS MY
MIND HOME ONCE MORE AND I STOP PICKING
AT OLD SCABS

WE ARE ALL FULL OF BATTLECRIES

481.
WE HAVE THE REST OF OUR LIVES
SO WHY NOT FUCKING START NOW?

482.
MY BONES SHATTER UNDER THE WEIGHT OF
MY DESIRE FOR YOU
WE ARE ONLY THIS MOMENT
AND EVERY NEXT MOMENT TO COME

483.
WE WISH FOR EACH OTHER WITH RECKLESS
ABANDON BETWEEN STRINGS OF PASSION,
HELLOS, GOODBYES
OUR HEARTS HOLD OUR FUTURES WITH THE
STRENGTH OF THE PLANETS
OUR DREAMS CHASE THE STARS AND I FIND,
WITH CERTAINTY, ALL GALAXIES LEAD BACK
TO YOU

484.

I FORGIVE THE UNIVERSE FOR THESE CARDS
DEALT

485.

I WAKE UP MOST DAYS AWASH IN THE
REMNANTS OF MY DREAMS
THE PASSION OF MY CONVICTIONS LEAVES
MY PILLOW SCORCHED WHEN I TURN MY
HEAD
BUT OTHER DAYS THE INFERNO COMES WITH
ME AS I WAKE AND THE VEIL OF THE TRANCE
DOES NOT LIFT

I THANK THE STARS UNLUCKY AND LUCKY
ALIKE, WITHOUT DISCRIMINATION, THAT MY
WOUNDS HAVE HEALED, WHILE SO MANY WILL
NOT

486.

AVENGING YOU IS THE MOST NOBLE CAUSE
MY HEART WILL EVER HOLD

487.
I OPEN MY EYES AND MY HEART CALLS OUT
FOR YOU
THE BONES OF MY SPIRIT ARE DESPERATE TO
SHARE MORE OF MYSELF WITH YOU, MORE
THAN YESTERDAY, SO THAT MY COMMITMENT
MIGHT MATCH THE EVER-GROWING SENSE OF
INFINITY IN MY CHEST
BUT MY SHARING IS LIMITED BY PAST
EXPERIENCES, DISTANCE, TIME
AND I AM QUICKLY RUNNING LOW ON NEW
MATERIAL

488.
PERHAPS THE ONLY DIFFERENCE BETWEEN
GODS AND DEMONS IS PERSPECTIVE
IF THAT IS EVEN A DIFFERENCE AT ALL

WE ARE ALL FULL OF BATTLECRIES

489.
SOULMATE [SOWL-MEIT]
NOUN.

a. MY FINGERS ACHE FOR LOVE AND REACH
    OUT, AND FIND YOU, MORE THAN I HAD
    HOPED, AND MY POEMS AND MY WORDS
    ARE LESS SIGNIFICANT THAN I WOULD
    LIKE. I FIND THAT, FACED WITH
    OVERWHELMING CONNECTION, I AM NOT A
    PATIENT WOMAN.

b. TWO SOULS MAKE A FAMILY.

c. I HAVE BEEN LONGING FOR YOU SINCE
    BEFORE I KNEW YOU, AND WITH YOU IN MY
    ARMS AND MY THOUGHTS I FIND THAT THE
    WORLD MAKES MORE SENSE THAN I HAD
    REALISED.

d. THERE IS WIND AND THERE IS RAIN AND
    MY BONES RATTLE. I THINK OF YOU AND
    THE WIND FEELS MORE LIKE A BREEZE
    AND THE RAIN BRINGS WILDFLOWERS AND
    I SIT IN A FIELD AND BREATHE IN
    SPRINGTIME AND I CALL OUT FOR YOU SO
    THAT WE MIGHT SHARE IT.

e. CHRIST, I LOVE YOU SO, AND WILL FOR ALL
    MY DAYS.

AMBER SELQET
CXCIX

490.
BEING ALIVE MATTERS QUITE A LOT WHEN I
HAVE SO MANY THOUGHTS LEFT TO SHARE

491.
THE AUTUMN LEAVES BRING FRESH
THOUGHTS
GENTLE EVENINGS AND APPLE PIES WITH MY
LOUD AND INDELICATE HEART
PROGRESS LOOKS DIFFERENT ON EVERYONE
BUT FOR ME IT LOOKS LIKE FRESH PAINT THE
WALLS
AND A PLACE WHERE I KNOW MY HEAD CAN
REST
TODAY, TOMORROW, A YEAR, A DECADE
THE UNIVERSE FEELS SOMEHOW INFINITE

AMBER SELQET
CC

492.

I THINK OF YOU IN COLOURS WHICH DO NOT
EXIST
I REINVENT THE WHEEL WITH WORDS AS I
REACH OUT TO FIND NEW WAYS TO EXPRESS
MY FEELINGS FOR YOU, WHO HOLDS MY
HEART
HARD WORK BORNE FROM OUR BONES -
INVENTION IS THE TRUEST PRODUCT OF LOVE

493.

I AM BATHED IN THE MILK OF THE MOON AND I
BITE INTO THE TOUGH FLESH OF AN AGED
SERPENT
PERHAPS IT WAS ONCE A GOD, BUT NOW IT IS
THE VANQUISHED IN THE HUNT
I WADE DEEPER INTO DESIRE AS BLACK
BLOOD DRIPS FROM MY ARMS, DOWN MY
CHEST, SLICK WITH PURPOSE
THE ORDER OF THE WORLD IS NOT EASILY
CHANGED
I WILL FORCE IT TO REMAKE WITH GORE AND
WICKEDNESS, FOR TWO CAN PLAY THIS GAME
I GIVE IN TO ALL THE VICES OF GLUTTONY AND
PLEDGE DEATH TO THE INADEQUATE
SOUR CHOICES STING MY NOSTRILS
FOR ONCE, THEY'RE NOT YOURS

AMBER SELQET
CCI

WE ARE ALL FULL OF BATTLECRIES

494.

SHE SINS, HE PAYS

AND, STILL, THE WORLD CONTINUES TO TURN
BECAUSE IN THE END IGNORANCE IS THE
GRAVEST TRANSGRESSION OF THEM ALL

495.

WITH A BLACK SCYTHE THE ALL-MOTHER
SLICES THE BEAST TO END THE REIGN OF
FEAR
WITH EACH DROP OF SCARLET FROM HIS
CHEST, TEN MORE MONSTERS SPRING TO
LIFE
IN ORDER TO DEFEAT HIM, THE GODDESS
CONSUMES HIS BLOOD
IN THE HOLD OF THE BLOOD DANCE, SHE
DOES NOT REALISE THE BATTLE HAS BEEN
WON
SACRED MADNESS HOLDS HER STEADY, AS
SHE DRINKS HER LOVER'S BLOOD
LUCIDITY, TOO LITTLE TOO LATE, AND SHE
SLICK WITH SHAME AND COVERED IN THE
STICKY REMINDER OF HER OWN SINS

A THOUSAND NIGHTS AND STILL THE WATER
SEEPING FROM HER SOUL WILL NOT WASH
CLEAR

AMBER SELQET
CCII

WE ARE ALL FULL OF BATTLECRIES

496.

WE STAND FIRM ON PROOF OF ETERNITY AND GAZE UPON FALLING WATER

OUR HANDS PROTECT ONE ANOTHER WITH GENTLE REMINDERS, *WE ARE HERE TOGETHER*

THE ROAR OF THE WATERFALL MATCHES OUR HEARTS, WHICH MURMUR SWEET FOREVERS

"I AM YOURS AND WILL STILL BE YOURS LONG AFTER THE RIVERS STOP FLOWING"

WE DECLARE WAR ON STAGNATION AND KISS ONE ANOTHER AS WE TAKE ON ANOTHER DAY, HANDS BOUND TOGETHER WITH RIBBON AND ENDURING VOWS

WE WERE DESIGNED TO SPEND OUR DAYS AS ONE

497.
"DARK HAIRED CHILD, EYES LIKE AN ECLIPSE,
SPARE AN EAR FOR THIS OLD CRONE"

"ANYTHING CAN HAPPEN CHILD, ALL
THOUGHTS CAN BE"

THE SEA NYMPH PUSHES MY HAIR BEHIND MY
EAR AND DISLODGES A BUTTERFLY THAT
SEEMS AS THOUGH IT WAS ALWAYS THERE. I
AM STANDING BETWEEN CRYSTALS AND SHE
IS FLOATING BETWEEN CLOUDS.

"BE SKEPTICAL OF ALL, MY LOVE"

A SINGLE TEARDROP OF EMERALD FALLS
FROM HER LASHES, AND WHERE IT HITS THE
OCEAN I FEEL IN MY SOUL THAT I HAVE
WITNESSED THE BIRTH OF A NEW
CONSTELLATION.

THE MOON IS TEN TIMES LARGER THAN IT
WAS BEFORE AND IT CRIES THE COLOURS OF
A DAYDREAM. THE BUTTERFLIES THAT ALWAYS
WERE HAVE MULTIPLIED AGAIN, AND THEY
FOLLOW THE OLD GOD BACK OUT TO SEA.

AMBER SELQET
CCIV

498.
IN THE WAKE OF MY DEVASTATION I FIND
RUTHLESS PASSION FOR LOVE, AND
UNWAVERING REJECTION OF COMPROMISE.
WE FALL, A JUMBLE OF LIMBS AND HOPES AND
DREAMS, TOGETHER INTO THE NIGHT.

WE ARE ALL FULL OF BATTLECRIES

499.
THE GRIM REAPERS LOOK LIKE SOFT SKIN
AND FLAMES AND DEMAND OF ME THE
PASSWORD

"SEVEN"

THEY LAUGH KNOWINGLY AND WAVE THEIR
HANDS TOWARDS THE SERPENT
I STARE AT FORGOTTEN SOULS AND CLOUDY
GLASS AND WONDER WHERE TO START
THERE IS AN ABUNDANCE OF THAT WHICH IS
FORGOTTEN, SO I TAKE MORE SOULS THAN I
AM OWED

DEATH CATCHES ME BEFORE I LEAVE AND
STARES PAST MY EYES AS WISDOM FLOWS
"IF YOU BITE MORE THAN YOU CAN SWALLOW,
ALL SOULS ARE WORSE OFF
WHATEVER YOUR INTENTIONS, IN TIME,
YOU'LL FORGET WHAT YOU'VE FORGOTTEN"

WE ARE ALL FULL OF BATTLECRIES

500.
WILD WITH DESPAIR, SHE HISSES AT THE
FORESTS AND SPITS ACID ONTO THE EARTH
THE SOIL ROTS WHERE SHE WALKS, CARVING
THE LAND IN TWO
HER CHILDREN WILL BE PROTECTED, FROM
GODS AND MEN ALIKE

501.
THE LINE BETWEEN MAN AND MONSTER
BLURS
I AM NOT A LEARNED MAN AND I CANNOT
BEGIN TO KNOW WHERE TO BEGIN
BUT I KNOW EVIL WHEN I SEE IT
AND I INTEND TO KEEP THE OCEANS
BETWEEN US TWO

WE ARE ALL FULL OF BATTLECRIES

502.
THE RIVER SOUNDS LIKE IDLE AFTERNOONS
AND VOYAGES HOME
I HEAR BEES AND THEY HEAR ME BUT WE
MAINTAIN OUR SEPARATE ORBITS, MINE
ALONGSIDE YOURS
OUR WORDS FRAME OUR HEARTS AND THE
MOMENT
WE SIT BETWEEN BLADES OF GRASS AND
DAYDREAMS, UPON HILLS OF FORGET-ME-
NOTS, AND MUSE UPON OUR COMMITMENT
"WHAT ARE WE GOING TO DO WITH ALL THIS
FUTURE?"
THERE IS LAZINESS IN OUR VOICES,
COMFORT IN CERTAINTY, AND GOSPEL WHERE
OUR SOULS INTERTWINE

WE ARE ALL FULL OF BATTLECRIES

503.
THE CONSTELLATIONS BETWEEN US BIND
OUR WRISTS AND KEEP OUR VOWS HONEST
DEATHS OF OLD STARS BRING NEW
CERTAINTY OF HEARTS AND FORTUNES
I READ OUR TAROTS AND THEY CONFIRM
WHAT I ALREADY KNEW IN OUR MIND
WE CREATE OUR OWN CARDS TO DEAL AND
IMBUE OUR ACTIONS WITH LOVE IN THE FORM
OF RESPONSIBILITY
WE STACK THE DECK WITH GOOD INTENTIONS
YOU COME HOME AND I AM GRATEFUL FOR
YOUR SAFE RETURN
I AM GRATEFUL EACH DAY, AGAIN
AND SO I SEND MY HEART AND MY THOUGHTS
WITH YOU WHEN YOU WALK OUT THE DOOR
COME BACK SAFE AGAIN, THANK YOU

WE ARE ALL FULL OF BATTLECRIES

504.
BLISTERED HANDS WHERE THEY MEET THE
SHOVEL
HE IS A SLAVE TO THE INEVITABLE
ANOTHER DAY, ANOTHER GRAVE

A BAT SOARS ABOVE AS THE EVENING BUGS
EMERGE
HE CONSIDERS THEM FRIENDS, OF SORTS,
COLLEAGUES
A CHUCKLE
AT LEAST HE WON'T HAVE TO BURY THEM

THE GRAVEDIGGER WISHES THE GODS WERE
REAL SO THEY'D TAKE PITY, AND GIVE HIM A
BREAK
PERHAPS THIS IS HIS PURGATORY
THERE HASN'T YET BEEN A DAY WITHOUT A
DEATH
HE WONDERS IF THE SUN CANNOT SET
WITHOUT SACRIFICE
OR MAYBE, IT JUST DOESN'T WANT TO

NATURE IS A FICKLE THING AND HE IS A MAN
WITH BILLS TO PAY
BRING IN THE BODIES
HIS DAY HAS JUST BEGUN

AMBER SELQET
CCX

505.

WE COME FROM BROKEN DREAMS
HOW WE GROW IS WHAT DEFINES US

506.

SAVE YOUR SINS FOR THE DIRTY MIRROR
WHEN IT'S 8PM
HOT SHOWERS AND CHAOTIC ROCK AND LUST
FILLED THOUGHTS
SURRENDER TO YOUR DESIRES WITH
RHYTHMIC HIPS AND DARK LIPS
THE BRUISES ON MY NECK AND MY THIGHS
TIE MY HUNGER TO YOU
I AM FUCKING INSATIABLE AND I NEED YOU
HERE NOW
I CONTINUE MY TANTRIC DANCE AND
PRETEND IT WILL SATISFY MY PRIMAL NEED
TO USE YOU

WE ARE ALL FULL OF BATTLECRIES

507.
YOU HAVE BEEN TOO BOLD AND I CAN SEE
THE REMNANTS OF YOU BLOSSOMING ON MY
NECK
I KNOW THE MARKS ARE TEMPORARY
I LONG FOR YOU TO RENEW YOUR CLAIMS ON
ME

508.
IT SEES ME, OH GOD IT SEES ME
COLOSSAL EYES THE COLOUR OF ANGER AND
THEY SEE ME
THERE IS NO HIDING AND I KNOW IT IN THE
VELVET INNARDS OF MY BONES
WE LOOK AT ONE ANOTHER AND I THINK
PERHAPS WE MAY UNDERSTAND ONE
ANOTHER, IN THE WAY THAT THE FOX
UNDERSTANDS A RABBIT
I AM OKAY WITH BEING PREY JUST AS LONG
AS I DO NOT KNOW IT

PLEASE LEAVE ME BE, PLEASE

*I AM CAPTIVATED BY THE REALISATION THAT
THE UNIVERSE DOES NOT NEED ME AND THE
FOX IS NOT HUNGRY AND I MUST CREATE MY
OWN REASON FOR BEING*

AMBER SELQET
CCXII

509.

YOU BRING ME TO MY KNEES IN THE WAY
THAT THE ANGELS ONLY SHOULD
I COMMIT UNHOLY ACTS AND YOU DO NOT
FIND IT AS FUNNY AS I DO
MY DEVOTION FEELS SPIRITUAL AS I GIVE IN
TO SHARED DEPRAVITY

510.

I AM CHOKING ON THE SUGAR IN YOUR
WORDS
MY BLOOD IS LIKE HONEY AND IT IS SLOW,
TOO SLOW, TOO SWEET
I AM A BEACON OF WEAKNESS AND I AM SURE
THAT THE AIR IS THICK WITH MY OWN DEMISE

WE ARE ALL FULL OF BATTLECRIES

511.
SUBTLE WOMAN NO MORE
HOLD ME AND TOUCH ME AND LOVE ME AND
TAKE ME AND USE ME AND NEED ME
I HAVE SO MUCH PASSION TO SHARE AND I
FEEL THAT I AM LOST AND ADRIFT ON A RAFT
IN THE MIDDLE OF THE PACIFIC AND ALL I
WANT IS TO KNOW WHERE I AM FOR A
MOMENT

AND A HUG, IF THERE'S ONE TO SPARE

512.
MOUTH FULL OF SORRY
MIND FULL OF FEAR
SHE WON'T SURVIVE THE NIGHT
ANOTHER EMPTY VESSEL CAUGHT ADRIFT

513.
SCALES DON'T MAKE A MONSTER
AND INTENTIONS DON'T MAKE A SAINT

AMBER SELQET
CCXIV

WE ARE ALL FULL OF BATTLECRIES

514.
PULVERISE THE LIARS WHERE THEY STAND
BETRAYED BY THEIR OWN CONSCIENCE
DESPITE THEIR BEST EFFORTS
EVEN THE GOD OF FORGIVENESS WILL NOT
ERASE THIS SIN

515.
THE SUN HAS NOT YET REACHED THE HARSH
HOURS BUT MY BLOODLUST IS AT ITS PEAK
I POUR MYSELF A SHOT OF VODKA AND
PRETEND IT IS YOUR KISS
I AM DRUNK ON THE THOUGHT OF OWNING
YOU AND SPITTING MY POISON INTO YOUR
MOUTH
THE ALCOHOL DOES NOT BURN THE WAY MY
ARM DOES WHERE YOU GRAZED YOUR
FINGERS ACROSS MY SKIN

516.
HE SHEDS HIS SKIN UNDER THE OAK IN THE
CLEARING AND COVERS HIMSELF IN FALLEN
LEAVES
THEY WILT LIKE THE LILY ON HIS WINDOWSILL
HE FORGOT TO WATER AGAIN
AUTUMN IS THE SEASON FOR HEARTBREAK
AND PRETENDING THE YEAR MIGHT NOT LAST
QUITE SO LONG

517.
I WELCOME YOU WITH OPEN ARMS INTO THIS
CAVITY I CALL A HOME
"SOMETHING SEEMS DIFFERENT"
IT'S ME, I'M MUCH MUCH WORSE

WE ARE ALL FULL OF BATTLECRIES

518.
WE ANSWER THE RAIN IN A HOWL MADE OF
ANGER
THERE ARE NO HALF PROMISES TONIGHT
WE WILL HUNT AS IF THE SKY WAS CLEAR AND
THE MOON WAS HIGH AND THE GODS WERE
SMILING
BECAUSE WE MUST
AND WE WILL <u>DIG DEEP</u> WITH OUR NAILS AND
BITE BONES WITH OUR JAWS AND SCREAM
MURDER WITH OUR LUNGS
BECAUSE WE CAN
AND GODDAMN,
WE REALLY FUCKING WANT TO

519.
PRAY, BEG FOR A FOX
RECEIVE YET ANOTHER HEN

WE ARE ALL FULL OF BATTLECRIES

520.
THE ALLEY IS COLD AND DARK AND DAMN
WITH POOR DECISIONS
YOU HAVE MADE THE MOST SIGNIFICANT OF
ALL THE POOR DECISIONS, JUST NOW, AND I
AM THE ONLY GOD HERE AND I AM NOT IN THE
HABIT OF MERCY

THIS BODY WAS MINE ALONE TO SHARE, AND
NOW YOUR BODY IS MINE ALONE TO DESTROY
PERHAPS YOUR KNEECAPS WILL BEND
BETTER WITH A LITTLE HELP

ASHES TO ASHES, MISTAKES TO REGRET

GIVE ME SOME SINS TO REPENT FOR SO AT
LEAST YOU'LL HAVE HALF A USE
THIS DAGGER IS BORNE OF MY BLOOD AND IT
DOESN'T TAKE A LARGE BLADE WITH A CHEST
SO SHALLOW AND A LITTLE BIT OF ELBOW
GREASE

THE DEBRIS OF OUR COLLISION SPLASHES
HIGH AND YOUR BLOOD TASTES SWEETER
THAN LAW AND ORDER EVER COULD

AMBER SELQET
CCXVIII

WE ARE ALL FULL OF BATTLECRIES

521.
IT HAS BEEN A LONG WINTER, PERHAPS A
LITTLE TOO LONG AND THE BEAST IS TIRED
THERE IS AN ARROW BETWEEN HIS FUR

"I WILL BE REBORN"

IF HE THINKS TOO HARD ABOUT IT THERE IS A
FOG, AND HE IS SURE HE DOES NOT HAVE A
CHOICE IN HIS FATE

"I WONDER WHEN I GET TO REST"

DROPS OF RED SEEP FROM THE ARROW'S
MARK AND MELT THE SNOW
THE CREATURE IS JEALOUS AND WISHES THAT
PERHAPS THE DIRECTION OF HIS ENDLESS
MONOTONY WOULD CHANGE TOO

522.
I SET MY BED ON FIRE WITH MY FINGERS
BETWEEN MY LEGS AND YOUR NAME
BETWEEN MY LIPS
I BURN MYSELF ALIVE IN ECSTASY AND FIND
MYSELF MORE DESPERATE FOR YOU THAN
BEFORE

AMBER SELQET
CCXIX

WE ARE ALL FULL OF BATTLECRIES

523.
IN ANOTHER UNIVERSE I CHOOSE TO BE KIND
AND GENTLE AND QUICK TO FORGIVE THE
SINS OF THE UNIVERSE
BUT THIS IS NOT HOW THINGS SHOULD BE
AND THIS TIME I HAVE CHOSEN TO BE KIND TO
MYSELF BECAUSE I DON'T OWE THE WORLD
BUT I DO OWE MYSELF A LIFE AND IF I DON'T
PICK ME, WHO WILL?

I TAKE MYSELF TO THE PARK AND BECOME
INFATUATED WITH A VERSION OF MYSELF
LONG AGO FORGOTTEN
THERE IS A BIRD IN THE TREES AND I CAN'T
QUITE SEE IT BUT EVERY NOW AND THEN A
RUSTLE REMINDS ME IT IS THERE
THERE'S A BOAT ON THE RIVER AND I PONDER
ON WHETHER I COULD BRIBE MY WAY ABOARD
I WONDER WHERE IT IS HEADED
I DON'T BELIEVE IT MUCH MATTERS

I DECIDE I SHOULD LEARN A FEW MORE
SKILLS ON THE OFF-CHANCE ONE OF THEM
GIVES ME THE EDGE MY BRIBERY NEEDS
HARD WORK FOR FREEDOM, A SIMPLE TRADE
THERE ARE STILL MORE BIRDS I'D LIKE TO
WATCH SING THROUGH THE BRANCHES ON
THE TREES

AMBER SELQET
CCXX

WE ARE ALL FULL OF BATTLECRIES

524.

I AM A LEVIATHAN CARVED FROM NECESSITY
EACH OF MY CLAWS IS A MONUMENT TO THE
UNFAIRNESS OF THIS EARTH

SAY IT ISN'T SO

THIS WORLD IS A FICKLE THING AND IF YOU
CAN'T BEAT THEM, THE LEAST YOU CAN DO IS
PUT UP A FIGHT

I AM SURE THAT THIS WAS ONCE A HOME BUT
NOW IT IS THE OBJECT OF MY DESPAIR AND I
LET IT FUEL MY BLOWS WITH RIGHTEOUS
INDIGNATION

I KNOW I AM A MONSTER BUT DENIAL IS THE
GENTLEST OF SINS AND I AM NOT YET READY
TO FACE THE TRUTH OF MY METAMORPHOSIS

I KNOW THAT I AM ANOTHER VILLAIN IN THIS
STORY
SOME VILLAINS ARE BORN OF CIRCUMSTANCE
I AM BORN OF YOU

AMBER SELQET
CCXXI

WE ARE ALL FULL OF BATTLECRIES

525.
HOPE IS THE TRADE OF THE CHAINED
WE BOTH KNOW THAT ALL CHAINS BREAK AND
LIBERATION IS INEVITABLE
AT LEAST YOU KNOW YOUR JAILER

I WILL KEEP YOU A LITTLE WHILE LONGER AS I
CHASE MY OWN DAMNATION

526.
THE SMELL OF LIQUID IRON AND UNCOATED
LUST HAILS SEALS MY SENSES IN OVERDRIVE
MY MOUTH TASTES LIKE COPPER AND
CURSES AND I CAST SPELLS I DON'T
REMEMBER LEARNING
I AM SPEAKING IN TONGUES FORGOTTEN
CENTURIES AGO AS THE CRACKS IN THE
DESERT SEAL SHUT
AN OASIS OF DEFIANCE SWALLOWS US UP
AND ALL MISDEEDS ARE EXPUNGED
THE REST OF THE WORLD CAN HANG FOR
ONE BRIEF MOMENT OF QUIET

SHHH

WE ARE ALL FULL OF BATTLECRIES

// **THE END** //

AMBER SELQET
CCXXIII

WE ARE ALL FULL OF BATTLECRIES

// WAGE WAR, MY WOLVES //

AMBER SELQET
CCXXIV